How and why do we learn?

HOW AND WHY
DO WE LEARN?

Edited by W. R. Niblett

FABER AND FABER

24 Russell Square

London

First published in mcmlxv
by Faber and Faber Limited
24 Russell Square London WC1
Printed in Great Britain by
Latimer Trend & Co Ltd Plymouth

Contents

7

Introduction

This book, which springs from a series of public lectures given in the session 1963–64 at the University of London Institute of Education, falls into two parts. The first is the work of six distinguished English psychologists, each with his contribution to make to the main theme and each aware of the importance of on-going research in his field. But it is to be noted that the amount of research done in a particular territory is not necessarily proportionate to the need. Stephen Wiseman notes that little research work has been done on the teaching of social attitudes and ideals. This kind of research is rare, owing, for one thing, to the infrequency with which anyone deliberately seeks to teach them in schools and for another to the difficulty of drawing a line neatly around any one attitude or ideal so as to separate it out from others that are akin to it.

Among the points most stressed in Part One of the book is the importance of environmental factors in learning. Yet here again the complexities are such that research has hardly yet begun to touch some of the main problems. Doris Lee illustrates one of them when she writes tellingly of the differences which background habits make to the very kinds of perception which will be possible to children: the little Africans she saw in the schools of Southern Rhodesia simply could not see what her simple pictures were about.

Any group to which a man deeply belongs has a far-reaching influence not merely upon what he will, but what he can, see or hear or learn. In childhood we learn much from our families and others without being conscious that we are doing so. 'Essentially we are beings,' says Ben Morris, 'who develop by means of our relationships with one another and are therefore in part constituted through these relation-ships.' Many kinds of learning will not take place at all in isolation from other people.

As children grow they learn to play roles that are in accordance with certain patterns of group expectation, but if they are to learn to live maturely with others, they must do more than simply play roles—they must become personally involved. 'To succeed in learning to live with one's neigh-bours is of little benefit if one can no longer live with one-self,' as William Taylor quietly remarks. Learning is not a matter of acquiring facts, skills and habits only but very much of absorbing an outlook and arriving at personal standards and values too. This is one of the central conten-tions of Part One of the book.

Part Two is made up of three very individual essays which at first sight seem to have but a tenuous connection with those that have preceded them. What on earth, it may be said, is a paper like Sir Hugh Foot's—passionate, con-cerned, intensely involved—doing at all in a book on How and Why Do We Learn? Why should such an individual essay as Stephen Potter's—personal, autobiographical, ex-periential—be found in it? Why even should Richard Hog-gart's protest against the methods of the advertisers be part of a series of lectures on learning?

These three contributions, in fact, illustrate the point made repeatedly in Part One that some essential kinds of learning cannot be done at all unless one is a member of a group which has deeply held values. All three are protests against a conventional, school-bound, concept of what learning is or should be. Unexamined routines of behaviour are subtle means of teaching conformity; and much teaching whether in the classroom or by the advertiser is implicitly conformist. These essays are at once a stimulus to enlarge our notions of 'learning' and an exemplification of how some kinds of learning have effectively been done.

Hoggart's main thesis is a specific illustration of points made in Part One: he argues that through advertisements we may be taught what kind of expectations we are to have from life as well as from things. That is one reason why they bring danger with them; and it is a danger we can only overcome if we are aware of it. How shall we learn to live the good life at all, if living is only an adjustment to the assumptions made by our society? The falsity of the 'palliness' of the T.V. advertiser exemplifies Morris's point that a group leader who is in the long run to be really educative must be the servant of the group, with its truer and deeper interests at heart.

All three of the final chapters suggest that much learning comes from experiences that occur after schooldays are over. Perhaps academics still underestimate the importance of life itself as a teacher. Potter and Foot provide unforgettable examples of how we learn to sense, to feel and to believe, examples not so much of learning *how* as of learning *that*. The great thing about both of them is their 'power to say "Look!" '—the one at the world within, the world of the imagination, the other at the world outside, whose problems go on so constantly defying us.

W.R.N.

PART ONE

1

STEPHEN WISEMAN

Learning versus teaching

The title of my lecture is 'learning versus teaching'. Of these three words, the most interesting is the second. It implies conflict, or opposition—and yet, we may ask, are these not the two sides of a single coin? Do they not refer to a single process, the differentiation merely lying in the point of view of the speaker, the direction of the process—like *giving* and *receiving*? Perhaps so. And yet the closer one looks at the matter, the more doubtful it appears. The relationship between these two terms seems to be far from simple, much less self-evident. My purpose in this lecture, the first of a series of nine, is to examine some aspects of this relationship, since, presumably, this is a matter which will be relevant to all the subsequent lectures. I shall do this by considering some of the research which has been done in this field, and the theories which have developed, and are developing, out of this experimental work. Nearly all of you in this hall are, no doubt, teachers of one sort or another. I need not emphasize to you that you bring to consideration of this problem a set of attitudes and beliefs, acquired during your professional life in all sorts of ways, and which are only partially grounded in established fact. These may lead you to certain biases in the weighing of the evidence; to an undue preference for one kind of theory at the expense of another. To take a very elementary example, and one immediately relevant to the title of my paper, consider how you view the results of an examination taken by your own students or pupils. For those at the top of the list, do you not—privately—preen yourself at this evidence of good *teaching*? And are not those at the bottom of the list mentally castigated for their failure in *learning*? Your lecturer himself is not immune from these biases: I can only suggest that an involvement in educational research for a considerable number of years has forced him to rearrange his prejudices rather more frequently than have most of his audience. I hope you will forgive me for stressing this matter of attitude and unconscious prejudice. Such factors are always at work, but in the present situation, where we wish to examine teaching and the teacher's role, their impact is likely to be all the greater, since some of my remarks may appear to be in conflict with your self-image as a professional person. Let me round off this little interpolated sermon with one of my favourite quotations: 'When, therefore, we find ourselves entertaining an opinion about the basis of which there is a quality of feeling which tells us that to inquire into it would be absurd, obviously unnecessary, unprofitable, undesirable, bad form, or wicked, we may know that the opinion is a non-rational one, and probably, therefore, founded upon inadequate evidence.'[1]

Let us begin by considering the psychology of learning, and learning theory. The literature here is enormous. Since the last war a great deal of experimental work has been carried out in this field. To find one's way around the mass of publications, to pick out the significant contributions, is far from easy. But the teacher finds himself bewildered and frustrated, not so much by the volume of work, but by the fact that the experiments conducted, the problems attacked, the theories advanced, seem to him to have little or no relevance to his own problems. The subjects of the experiments are not children, but rats and pigeons, dogs and dolphins. The 'learning' studied is learning of a very special and elementary kind. And, worst of all, in none of these experiments does a teacher ever appear! It is not surprising that, in

[1] W. Trotter, quoted by C. D. Hardie, *Background to Modern Thought*, Watts & Co., 1947, p. 117.

spite of the importance claimed for this work by psychologists, in spite of the prestige of some of the workers in this field, the teacher concludes that all this is irrelevant to school learning and the education of children. In this conclusion he is, at least partially, wrong. It is true that there is little *immediately* relevant to the classroom, but he is witnessing the slow development of a corpus of knowledge which, eventually, is likely to form part of the foundations of a comprehensive theory of children's learning. The pure psychologists have been concerned with the lowest levels of learning—sensori-motor learning—and have already uncovered the basic mechanisms involved here, in the achievement of goals, the conditioning of responses, the development of perception. The teacher is concerned mainly with learning involving explanation, understanding relationships, the recognition of truth, the development of attitudes. The study of animal learning gives us little direct help here: its relevance to the development of the new-born infant is more obvious. But it is wrong for the teacher and the educationist to underrate the importance of such work. Nor is it right to exclude some consideration of it from courses in teacher training, partly because of its relevance to the study of child development, but mainly because of its influence on the growing edge of knowledge, and of the inevitability of its place in the warp and woof of the final fabric of educational theory.

It would be wrong if I gave the impression that all experimental work in the psychology of learning has been done with animals. A great deal has involved children, and to some of this work we may now turn. For the very young child, the study of learning is the study of development: in many ways the terms are synonymous. Psychologists have studied child development ever since psychologists existed. Some of us here may have been brought up on Stanley Hall's 'race-recapitulation' theory, which suggested certain phases in the development of the child which paralleled the development of the race from primitivism to civilization. The next level of sophistication came with workers like Gesell, who laboriously carried out studies of developmental behaviour, and arrived at norms of progress. From Hall's speculative theory we thus arrived at factual data: a considerable achievement. But in neither case was there any attempt at *explanation*. As I have said elsewhere, referring to Hall's theory: 'This was an interesting speculation, and one which was admirably adapted as the basis of a lively student essay, but in its usual form it was of no value as a *theory*. It did nothing to explain *why* children did certain things at certain times, but merely gave a spurious respectability to the assertion "a child does so-and-so because he is a child".' (Wiseman, 1959, p. 133.) And Hunt (1961) has commented '. . . in Gesell's normative schedules, which are based upon the assumption of predetermined development, normative description is conceived to be the equivalent of explanation' (p. 168).

But both these comments are, perhaps, less than fair. There is an explanation, a theory, lying behind the work of Hall and Gesell and their followers, albeit an implicit one. Both these writers were powerfully influenced by the concept of heredity, and the notion that the process of child development consisted of the gradual unfolding of powers and abilities predetermined and pre-existing. From such a view-point came the concept of *maturation* which has played so powerful a part in theory. Stemming in the first instance from the work of biologists like Coghill (1929) experimental work on children soon gave supporting evidence. Gesell, for example, using identical twins and studying such activities as stair-climbing, showed that training in such skills was largely a waste of time. 'There is no conclusive evidence that practice and exercise ever hasten the actual appearance of such types of reaction as stair-climbing and tower-building with blocks. The time of appearance is fundamentally determined by ripeness of the neural structures . . . training does not transcend maturation' (Gesell and Thompson 1929). The teacher, then, is unnecessary—except, perhaps, as a passive agent providing opportunity for practice once the necessary level of maturation has been reached. The effect of such experiments on educational thought was powerful, coinciding as they did with an enormous interest in the study of individual differences and a climate of opinion which stressed the genetic basic of human talents and abilities. The effect on educational practice was slower and less apparent —partly, no doubt, because of the almost instinctive reluctance of teachers to embrace a theory which so radically curtailed their professional role and power. One of the outcomes of the movement was the production of *reading-readiness tests*, based on the claim that a mental age of 6½ years represented the maturation level required before the formal teaching of reading could hope to succeed. The fact that such tests are mentioned much more frequently in textbooks of educational psychology than they are seen in actual use in the classroom is perhaps evidence of the lack of professional conviction that I have already mentioned. The way in which the tests were—and are—used by those who accept them forms an interesting comment on the advantages and the dangers in this approach. Almost always such tests are used negatively: i.e. to identify those children who are not yet ready for formal teaching. And there is no doubt that much preventible backwardness may be avoided in this way, by safeguarding duller children from the stultifying effects of early failure. But how often are the tests used *positively*, to discover those children who are ready to learn long before they reach the magic chronological age of 6½?

But the main difficulty with the maturation theory is that it is too simple—and based on experiments that were too simple. Practice, and learning, were conceived too narrowly. Later work, examining the effects of deprivation of experience on young children, shows that such deprivation can have widespread effects, and delay maturation in performances which appear to be quite different. Dennis (1960),[1] for example, studying children in an orphanage in Teheran, where deprivation was extremely severe, found

[1] Quoted by Hunt (1961).

only 42 per cent of infants able to sit alone in their second year (Shirley's norm is 7 months) and only 8 per cent walking alone at the end of the third year (norm 15 months). Even more interesting is McGraw's (1935) historic study of the twins, Johnny and Jimmy. Johnny was allowed to practise roller skating at 11 months, when he was learning to walk. He was skating with skill at 16 months. Jimmy was kept from roller skating until he was 22 months old. After two and a half months' practice he failed to acquire any facility whatever. It seems possible, then, that by withholding experience at certain critical periods of development, later performance is permanently lowered. Hunt (1961) suggests: 'every period along the line of development must be critical for experience with certain types of circumstance' (p. 270). The maturation theory, then, represents an over-simplification; a lack of appreciation of the importance of motor and cognitive experience, and the richness of this, in determining maturation levels; and a failure to recognize the possibility of the irreversibility of some effects of deprivation of experience. But a more general effect must also be noted, an effect on the climate of opinion in educational practice. This led to an overstress of the dangers of premature teaching, an overstress of the importance of 'adjustment', and, by generalization, a denigration of intellectual achievement. In Fowler's (1962) words: 'In harking constantly to the dangers of premature cognitive training, the image of the "happy", socially adjusted child has tended to expunge the image of the thoughtful and intellectually educated child' (p. 145).

Let us now turn to a psychologist whose work over the last forty years has been instrumental in restoring the importance of cognitive development and intellectual education. I say 'psychologist', but this is less than accurate. His main associate (Inhelder 1953) has described him as 'a zoologist by training, an epistemologist by vocation, and a logician by method' (p. 75). I refer, of course, to Piaget. There is no doubt that both the teacher and the educationist see Piaget's researches and theories as more relevant and more understandable than those of any other psychologist in the field of learning. Over the last decade his work has come to have more and more impact, not only on educators, but also on other psychologists. Teachers who have never heard of Thorndike or Hull, Köhler or Tolman, are familiar with his name—even though they would be hard put to it to outline his theories! Some have a vague idea that he spends his time pouring water from a jug into beakers of various shapes and sizes for the edification of his own children, or playing with eggs and egg-cups. A more sophisticated group—such as my present audience—will know that he has attempted to chart the intellectual development of children from birth to adolescence, and has identified and described various stages in this development corresponding to increasingly complex logical processes. Notice the similarity of this end-result to the recapitulation theory of Stanley Hall, and the concept of maturation levels. And for the practising teacher, who has a smattering of the stage-structure but no appreciation of the theory and philosophy lying behind it, exactly the same dangers are present. It can be used as an excuse for restricting experience and diluting curriculum, as a justification for the offer of pap instead of grit, as a reason for cramping instead of stretching pupils. But such action is impossible for anyone who has read more than the first sentence in Piaget's score of published books. For him, development is produced by the interaction of the child and his environment, through the processes of 'assimilation' and 'accommodation'. In this way the rudimentary and elementary *schemata* of the infant become differentiated and co-ordinated into the logical organizations of the adult. In Piaget's own words 'life is a continuous creation of increasingly complex forms and a progressive adaptation of these forms to the environment' (Piaget 1936, p. 3). Although in a later book he points out that 'all interaction with the environment involves both a structuring and a valuation . . . we cannot reason, even in pure mathematics, without experiencing certain feelings, and conversely, no effect can exist without a minimum of understanding or of discrimination' (Piaget 1947, p. 6), nevertheless almost all his work is concerned with the *intellectual* aspects of development, rather than the motivational. In this he differs from Hebb (1949); Hunt (1961) comments: 'Piaget makes little of his observations and pronouncements about motivation, while Hebb has motivation near the centre of his concern' (p. 357). The more new stimuli and new experiences—of a complexity appropriate to the stage of development—the child accepts, the more zest he will have for yet newer experiences; the more new skills he masters, the greater his capacity for mastery. Individual differences in rate of development have received little attention from Piaget, mainly because of his relative unconcern for motivation, and this has led to a good deal of criticism. It is heartening to see other workers in different countries repeating his experiments on larger and more heterogeneous samples.

Another curious lopsidedness in Piaget's work is the lack of emphasis on environmental factors. Since development comes about through interaction with the environment, it might be imagined that studies of children with very different environmental histories would yield significant data. Piaget has charted a series of landmarks in intellectual development: what differences are observable in the average ages of passing these landmarks for normal children on the one hand, and deprived children on the other? What kind of deprivation appears most potent in its effects, physical, emotional, socio-familial? Answers to these questions would be of the greatest importance to teachers, and might lead us to highly significant discoveries about the complexities of child-environment interaction.

Since I have embarked on what must seem to you—with some justification—the somewhat arrogant and presumptuous task of criticizing Piaget for his sins of omission, perhaps I might round this off by mentioning just one more. And this—for my purpose tonight—is probably the most fundamental. I refer to his apparent lack of concern for the teacher and the role of the teacher. This, of course, is implicit in what I have already said. The teacher is vitally concerned with motivation, and is responsible for the control of the child's immediate environment—both intellectual and emotional. Any productive interaction between child and environment only occurs when there is a *match* between the child's existing *schemata* and the characteristics and demands of the environmental circumstances. Hunt (1961) comments: 'Piaget often remarks on the importance of basing educational practice on the natural phases of the child's interaction with the environment . . . [but] he fails to formulate the principle directly or to clarify it. In a sense, this principle is only another statement of the educator's adage that "teaching must start where the learner is", but it is poorly understood (p. 267–8) . . . the matching process is essentially a matter of empirical trial and error' (p. 272). Motivational and intellectual factors are inextricably tied up in this matching process. Harlow (1949) points out that learning 'sets' which underlie intelligent behaviour do not come ready made, as the Gestalt school believed, but must be acquired. The 'sets' of Harlow, Duncker and Hebb are similar to the 'strategies' of Bruner, the 'information processing technique' of the programmers, and have some interesting analogies in Guildford's factor analysis of creativity. One cannot imagine capitalizing on such discoveries without the intervention of a skilful and knowledgeable teacher. There are signs, however, of some redress of balance by practical teachers: for example, the 'inquiry training' of Suchman (1960 a & b), the pedigree of which might be described as 'by Piaget out of Socrates'.

Let us now look a little closer at one of the factors which Piaget has neglected: the environment itself. A great deal has been written—some of it in very purple prose—about the relative effects of heredity and environment on measured intelligence. I must resist the temptation to embark on this topic, and confine myself to considering the effects of environment on educational attainment. Much less has been

done on this, since it does not arouse so intensely the philo-
sophical and political passions associated with the 'IQ con-
troversy'. But what has been done shows pretty clearly that
environmental factors have a greater influence on educational attainment than they have on measured intelligence.
One of the most recent, and most thorough, investigations
demonstrating this is Fraser's (1959) survey in Aberdeen. A
survey of research in this field also reveals two significant
facts: first, that almost all investigations examine the re-
tarding effects of bad environment—we have practically no
research on the stimulating effects of good environment;
second, that a great deal of the work has been limited to
physical and economic conditions, and very little has been
done on the social attitudes and ideals of different groups.

Following the publication of the *Early Leaving* report
(1954) by the Ministry of Education, which showed a strong
connection between premature withdrawal from grammar
school and the social class of the parents, a good deal of
further work has been done along the same lines. The best
known is perhaps that of Floud, Halsey and Martin (1957)
working in S.W. Hertfordshire and Middlesbrough. This
research not only underlined the connections between social
class and school progress, but also revealed significant differences between the two areas under investigation. This
'geographic factor' was also shown by one of my own students
(Derrick 1961) in comparing grammar schools in Lancashire
and Dundee. The research-variable *social class* has exerted a
powerful magnetism on research workers, in spite of the frequent demonstration that it is too coarse and too unreliable
a measure to yield any significant insights into the mechanisms
underlying the interaction between environment and educational progress. The differences within any single one of the
amorphous 'social classes' are demonstrably much greater
than the differences between them, and it is these intraclass
differences that are the most important. Fraser (1959) found,
for example, significant discrepancies here, particularly for
the children of highly-skilled parents. She comments: 'As a

group, they are less intelligent than the children in the "clerical" group but yet are more successful in school' (p. 51). What seems to matter more than social class is parental encouragement. Pidgeon (1959) in reviewing work done by the National Foundation for Educational Research claimed that 'the most important factor bearing on the educational progress of all those so far investigated was the attitude of the child's parents'. We know more about this aspect of environment with respect to the development of infants than to that of school-age children. Murphy (1944) points out that the effects may work in opposite directions at different stages: 'In infancy, the protective mother may give the child a great deal of satisfaction if she is the kind that is protective because she is fond of babies. . . . But at the age of expanding loco-motion and exploration the over-protective mother becomes an inhibitor and deprives the child of opportunities which he needs to use his new abilities' (p. 658). The blanket concept of 'maternal deprivation' has, like that of social class, acted as a brake on research in recent years. Casler (1961) in a critical review of the literature, suggests that an hypothesis of *perceptual* deprivation—including tactile deprivation—is often a preferable one to that of maternal deprivation, while Hunt (1961) suggests that house-proud parents may well succeed in hampering the development of their children, and even lowering their final level of intelligence, by curtailment of their activity. He goes on to consider development beyond infancy, and concludes: 'Parental behaviours are very probably much more important determinants of rates of development than are such traditional indices of intellectual environment as level of parental education, socio-economic level, number of books in the house, etc. In fact, these traditional indices of intellectual environment may be very poor indicators of the behaviours which are important determiners.' (p. 314).

In the early years of infancy, it is easy to see how parental attitudes may have a profound effect on the quality and range of infantile experience and so affect the time and ease of attainment of Piaget's stages of intellectual development. But it is not so easy to see the underlying mechanism as the child grows older, a difficulty which leads Glidewell (1961) to suggest that future investigations should attempt to find links between attitude and behaviour. The effect on the child of strong parental attitudes leading to the rejection of selective secondary education and of higher education, or premature withdrawal from school, is obvious; but more subtle (and more important, perhaps) are those which affect the child's own attitude to school and the learning process. The undoubted affective basis of such mechanisms emphasizes the hiatus in Piaget's work caused by his lack of concern with motivational factors.

It should be noticed that effects such as these appear to be widespread over the civilized world. They exist in the comprehensive American high school as well as in the tripartite British system. A recent investigation in Egypt (Ismail 1963) shows that 'parental aspiration for college education for specific professions is much higher in the middle class'. Keeping up with the Jones's in material possessions is paralleled by an equivalent process of 'keeping down with the Smiths' culturally and educationally, to use McMahon's (1962) graphic phrase. No amount of tinkering with the organization of secondary education will make any fundamental change in environmental forces such as these. Indeed, it is possible that by seeking to reduce the overt 'injustices' of 11 + selection we may only succeed at the price of increasing the covert forces of anti-educational attitude. Many grammar school headmasters are familiar with the brilliant boy from the poor home, entering grammar school at eleven in spite of the indifference or even hostility of his parents, who look forward only to his leaving at 15 and beginning to earn. Continuing success at school gradually brings a degree of parental involvement and of parental education. Parent-child inter-action is a two-way process. By the time he reaches 15 they have so far modified their views as to permit him to continue to G.C.E. O-level. A resounding success here may complete the educational process and the parents become as anxious as the boy to see him go still further. I am not suggesting that this always happens, or even in the majority of cases. Yet it should be noticed that Crawford (1929) in the U.S.A., and Dale (1952) and Furneaux (1961) in this country, have failed to establish any connection between social class and academic attainment at the stage of entry to university. This suggests that the process of parental education reaches a critical phase about the time of G.C.E. If the parents have been won over by this stage, their support seems assured. What will happen to this kind of mechanism under the Leicestershire plan? The possibilities of parental education and the modification of their attitudes seem very much reduced. More than is gained on the swings may be lost on the roundabouts.

The complexities of the inter-action between environment and educational attainment have hardly, as yet, been touched by research. One of the most interesting aspects of this is the differential effect of environmental factors on the various sectors of educational attainment. In almost every research attainment has been treated as a single entity, and yet is it not likely that the verbal sector of learning may interact with experiential and environmental factors rather differently from, say, the mathematical or practical sectors? The first tentative beginnings of the investigation of such possible differences have been made in Manchester, in a series of researches begun in 1951 and which, as yet, are still unpublished.[1] Working with boys and girls of 14+, and using quite large samples (13,000 in 1951, 1,500 in 1957) we have correlated some twenty social variables with scores on tests of verbal intelligence, reading comprehension and mechanical arithmetic, investigating the distribution of backwardness and brightness as well as of average score. A factor analysis brings out a strong *ed: soc.* factor accounting for two-thirds of the total test variance, but it is the two

[1] Now published in Wiseman, S., 1964, *Education and Environment*, Manchester Univ. Press.

27

additional factors that provide the more interesting data (Wiseman 1964, table 7.11). The second factor differentiates the reading test from the other two, and shows that high performance in reading comprehension is associated with a low birth-rate, a high rate of immunization against whooping cough and diphtheria, low incidence of cases of cruelty and neglect, of action by the N.S.P.C.C. and of cases of probation under the age of 14. The third factor is one which does not differentiate between the three tests, but between the three methods of measuring competence, separating out *brightness* as a single entity. Brightness and backwardness are *not*, apparently, the obverse and reverse of a single coin. To put it in another way, if the regions of a city are ranked on the basis of the incidence of backwardness, those with little backwardness are not necessarily those with the greatest amount of brightness. Areas with low proportions of brightness are those with many cases of probation (14–16 years), of cleansing notices and verminous conditions, of scabies and of cruelty and neglect of children.

Both these factors may be thought of as factors of parental or maternal care. The differentiation appears to lie in the particular aspects of this. Reading seems to be associated with the factor concerned with the *psychological*, as opposed to the physical, aspect of maternal care, whereas the 'brightness' factor has heavy loadings on the 'dirt' variables, the *physical* aspect. The contrast fits in well with Wofinden's (1950) description of children from problem families in Bristol: 'These children are often verminous, suffering from impetigo, ill-clad and ill-shod, dirty and generally neglected, frequently absent from school with consequent prosecutions of the parents, but, withal, generally happy.'

It is clearly premature to try to explain such findings in terms of learning theory, whether we lean on Piaget or Pavlov, Thorndike or Thurstone. But extensions of such investigations—particularly with the primary school child—should yield significant insights, not only for the theoretician but also for the teacher in the classroom.

This reminds me that, according to the title of my paper, I am concerned with teaching as well as learning, and that so far I have said very little indeed about teaching and about the teacher. Since I started by saying that I would base my remarks on existing research findings, the fact that I am now well past my half-way mark indicates pretty clearly that the amount of research that has been done on teachers and teaching is very much smaller than that done on learning. A good deal of work has investigated the relative effectiveness of different teaching methods, but this is far less in volume than one would expect in view of the apparent importance and the immediate relevance of this to the teacher's job. And it is perhaps not unfair to say that a very high proportion of the work done has been of doubtful value, while of the remaining researches many have proved mutually contradictory. One of the reasons for this unhappy state of affairs is the fact that severe methodological problems face the research worker in this field. One of the many endemic difficulties is the impossibility, in nearly all experiments, of assigning teachers at random to different methods. Thus the effects of teaching ability become confounded with the effects of different methods—and few observers doubt the existence of significant inter-action here, that some teachers are more effective with one method, others with another. The intelligent enthusiast with a new teaching method is a particular hazard. He can often demonstrate that he himself can produce spectacular gains by its use. But the real question is whether this method, used by run-of-the-mill teachers of a heterogeneous sample of classes, can be shown to be significantly superior to more traditional methods. Another difficulty, often overlooked in the past, is the existence of what might be called the educational Hawthorne effect. If an experiment is set up, and experimental classes are given new and novel equipment and materials, are visited by friendly and interested strangers, are stimulated to work harder and work better, and are made aware, day after day, that they are engaged in something 'special' which sets them apart

29

from other classes, then achievement and competence are certain to improve. The presence of a so-called 'control group' which is merely another class of children of the same age and level of ability, pursuing the normal, work-a-day, run-of-the-mill programme, may give an air of academic respectability to the exercise, but this is wholly spurious: the control group must itself have equivalent intellectual and emotional stimulation, using material and method different from the experimental group, but also different from the familiar material and method.

I have picked out two of the many methodological difficulties facing the research worker, and these are perhaps the two most important. But the main reason for the disappointing results from experiments on teaching method is, I believe, more fundamental. It is the absence, from a large proportion of them, of any underlying theoretical concepts or hypotheses which would anchor them to the main framework of the psychology of learning. Experiments are not conceived within the context of learning theory, but are merely attempts to test the personal hunches of the experimenters. Advancement in understanding, or even improvement in teaching technique, are unlikely to result from such an approach. The impact of Piaget's work has, however, produced a salutary change, and more and more researches are being planned to answer questions arising from theory rather than from hunches. Perhaps this may be accounted one of Piaget's greatest contributions to education.

A survey of teaching method research suggests only one major conclusion at this stage of the development of our educational understanding: that particular methods are not as important as are the psychological factors operating in the teacher and in the pupil. Some teachers are better with one method than with another; some are better with dull pupils than with bright; no one is equally good—or bad—at teaching all aspects of his subject, or dealing with the whole range of classroom problems. Ought we not, therefore, to investigate the individual differences among teachers as assiduously as we examine the individual differences among children? This would certainly seem to be an aspect of the learning process just as worthy of study as methods of teaching, and one that is just as promising for productive insights. And yet a survey of work in this field over the last fifty years reveals an unimpressive and scanty record of sporadic and ill-co-ordinated researches, contributing little to our understanding of the qualities—intellectual and temperamental—which go to make a good teacher. Consequently, our methods of student selection and of teacher training are based on tradition and on opinion rather than what we *know* to be necessary for the production of an effective teaching force. We are at the mercy of current opinion—which can oscillate alarmingly from one educational fashion to another—and the most persuasive of the vast company of academic demagogues.

One of the biggest stumbling blocks here is the identification of a valid criterion of teacher quality and teaching success. I have no time to describe the various attempts to set up such a criterion,[1] but a survey of the field leads to one inescapable conclusion: that any attempt to set up a *single* criterion is foredoomed to failure. Even the most obvious and, to the Americans at least, perhaps the most persuasive criterion—that of pupil achievement—is not exempt. Hunt (1961, p. 275) describes a private school with a progressive approach to the nursery school and kindergarten programmes, giving children a width and richness of experience in number rather than formal teaching and mechanical drill. But achievement tests in later years showed *all* children in the bottom tenth at the first grade level, all in the bottom quarter in the second grade, all below average in the third grade. It was not until the fifth grade that the children, without exception, were found in the top third of the norm distribution. The true effectiveness of many of our best teachers is not seen immediately, but is all the more pervasive because of this. Teaching is too complex an activity for its

[1] But see Evans (1961), Wiseman (1962) and Allen (1963) for reviews of this.

quality to be expressed in a single measure. The most comprehensive research up to date—that of Ryans (1960)—although restricted to examination of the teacher inside the classroom, and thus ignoring very important aspects of professional competence and educative influence, underlines this conclusion. He identifies three principal dimensions, or criteria, of 'teacher behaviour', three factors that are independent aspects of teaching success: warmth of relationship with children; responsible and systematic organization; and originality and enthusiasm. The Manchester School of Education has embarked on a long-term programme of teacher research, and preliminary results are both interesting and disturbing. Using a sample of 247 teachers with six years' experience, we have compared two criteria of success: the amount of promotion achieved, and the opinion of the head teacher as revealed in a confidential reference. These two measures turn out to be independent and uncorrelated. But worse is to come. Promotion appears to be unconnected with teaching ability, whatever type of school the teacher is in. Intellectual qualities are similarly unimportant: indeed, in the primary school they appear to be a positive handicap! Almost the only quality that matters for promotion in the secondary modern school appears to be organizing ability, while for the primary school teacher extra-mural activity is what leads to advancement (Wiseman 1962 and 1963). No clearer indication could be given of the fact that the role of the teacher is seen very differently by those within the profession on the one hand, and those outside it, like school managers and members of governing bodies, on the other. And if the teacher's role as seen by the teacher trainers is different again from both of these, then the products of our training colleges will certainly not be viewed with enthusiasm by the schools, and the adjustments demanded of the newly qualified teacher will be all the more severe. It seems likely that the politician and the educational administrator each has his own 'brand image' of the teacher: if these differ markedly from those of the teacher himself the resultant educational planning, organization and legislation are unlikely to receive much professional acclaim or support. This confusion is not confined to schools. Sanford (1962) in his stimulating work *The American College*, writing of university teachers, says: 'Social scientists may see the proper role of the teacher as that of intellectual leader of his time, but large sections of the general population see it as a channel through which information is passed, a role that is best filled by "those who can't *do*" ' (p. 53).

The self-image of the teacher, and what he conceives his own role to be, no doubt varies from individual to individual, and may be profoundly affected by the type of school he is in, but it also seems to vary temporally. A recent American analysis of the contents of children's readers (de Charms and Moeller, 1962) suggests that 'there is a marked curvilinear relationship over time in the pressure put upon children for achievement. The evidence suggests an increase in achievement pressure from 1800 to 1890, a steady decrease thereafter through the 1940's, and other evidence indicates a recent increase again in the last few years' (Kuhlen 1963, p. 117). Perhaps similar changes are evident in our own culture? And if so, it would not be surprising if they paralleled a wider trend noted by Burt: 'In psychology as in politics, the pendulum of fashion swings to and fro; and the vacillations roughly synchronize. During the nineteenth century, the associationists preached an egalitarian doctrine, and three reform bills were passed. Then the close of the century witnessed a reaction; and we ourselves are witnessing the counter-reaction. An excessive emphasis on heredity has now been succeeded by an equally excessive emphasis on environment. Apparently it is difficult to give due weight simultaneously to each' (Burt, 1955, p. 167 n.).

It will be obvious that I am assuming that the quality of the teacher's self-image will affect his attitude to his pupils, the relative emphases he places on the various aspects of his work, and the goal towards which his professional activities are oriented. Examination of the 'role of the teacher' is

C

33

merely one other way of examining an important constellation of forces within the educational environment of the pupil. One of the most significant researches of the past decade is that of Stern (1962) working in the field of American college education. Using Murray's terminology of 'need' and 'press'—the needs of students and the press of their college environment—he has devised the *College Characteristic Index*, a diagnostic tool intended to reveal the value system underlying the rules and regulations, written and unwritten, of individual educational establishments. He finds that 'the vast majority of institutions examined thus far are characterized by environments that emphasize some degree of conformity and constraint' (p. 726). He finds the level of 'intellectual press' generally lower than that emphasizing good human relations, but major exceptions to this pattern 'are the small but *élite* private liberal arts colleges, which appear to be distinguished by their high level and breadth of the intellectual press and emphasis on personal freedom and informality' (loc. cit.). Later work has demonstrated extremely high correlations between level of intellectual press and academic achievement—a result not easy to interpret fully, since the quality of educational climate in an institution may affect profoundly the quality of applicant seeking admission. But it is clearly evident that we have here a line of attack that merits extension downwards into the secondary school and primary school, and that promises to yield new insights into the psychology of the learning process, particularly from the motivational aspect.

The time has come for me to round off these discursive and, I fear, ill-co-ordinated remarks by attempting some measure of integration. 'Learning versus Teaching': are they in apposition or opposition? What is the teacher's role? The large gaps in our knowledge, the lack of a comprehensive theory of learning, make the answers to such questions hazardous and inevitably tentative. There seems no doubt that many children—and particularly those of high intelligence—often learn in spite of their teachers rather than because of them.

Those of us who cling to the image of the teacher as a didactic figure, engaged in the skilful and patient unfolding of a logical sequence of facts and ideas, would be better advised to abandon this traditional concept. The teacher's role should rather be seen as that of a controller and manipulator of the intellectual environment, providing experience appropriate to the needs and potentialities of his pupils. The knowledge and skills and attitude demanded of the teacher for the successful prosecution of his function depend very considerably upon the age of his pupils, their intellectual powers, and the richness or paucity of their previous environmental experiences. Whether our training programmes prepare students adequately to fill this role is a moot point: as yet we have little or no factual evidence one way or the other. I suspect, however, that our efficiency is far from high. It is possible that the level of 'intellectual press' in many training colleges is below the threshold of tolerance, the inevitable result being that too high a proportion of teachers in primary and secondary modern schools fail to stimulate and extend their pupils' intellectual powers by providing sufficiently challenging material. I fancy, too, that in spite of what we know of the adverse educational effects of home and neighbourhood environment, our trainee teachers often have little grasp of the implications of this for their professional jobs. We do not know how far, nor in what ways, schools can successfully offset such effects. At present, those few children who successfully triumph over these powerful adverse forces appear to do so almost by accident. A more comprehensive system of educational guidance, with adequately trained teachers, might reap a rich harvest here. As Himmelweit has said, '. . . the boy from an unskilled working-class home needs special support; his parents need more guidance by discussing with them their uncertainties as seen from their, and not from the teacher's, frame of reference. Equality of opportunity does not come from ignoring differences which exist, by pretending they are not there, but by compensating for them' (Himmelweit 1963, p. 22).

35

In this survey of some of the research on learning and teaching I have tended, perhaps, to emphasize the gaps in our knowledge rather than the substantial gains we have made. It may present, to some of you, a depressing picture. Such a reaction would be wrong. After all, in spite of the fact that we have schools with traditions going back many centuries, in spite of the fact that most teachers take for granted that they are in a profession with a long history behind it— and therefore conclude that existing methods and organizations *must* be pretty sound—in spite of all these things we are, in fact, mere children at this complex job of providing universal education. We have only been at it for a mere fifty years or so. In the perspective of the history of man's civilization this is barely the wink of an eye. It is not surprising, then, that we make mistakes, that we don't know all the answers. My own view-point is one of optimism: qualified optimism, but nevertheless optimism. I see a number of developments that, taken together, provide more significant promise for progress than we have seen at any time since the 1944 Act. First is the astonishingly wide interest of teachers and educationists in the work of Piaget and his school. I hope that this is more than a fashion, that it denotes not only a recognition of the practical relevance of his work, but also a resurgence of belief that the basic task of education is that of *intellectual* development. Second, and undoubtedly related to this, is the almost explosive nature of activity and interest in the field of curriculum development. This applies at all levels of education, but particularly, perhaps, to the primary school. I am thinking particularly of developments in the teaching of science, of mathematics, and of modern languages. Here there is a real wind of change blowing, and one with enormous potentialities. As one who, in another capacity, acts as an educational entrepreneur, providing in-service courses for teachers, I can assure you that in this field we are quite unable to keep pace with the demand. Two years ago, only a handful of mathematics teachers had ever heard the term 'set theory'. Now, there are literally hundreds engaged on

36

the demanding task of, first, learning it, and second, devising methods of teaching mathematics from this orientation. And this example can be paralleled in other subjects. The third development I see which nourishes my optimism is one which may prove in the long run to be more significant than any other for future progress. I refer to the provision by the Ministry of Education, for the first time, of money for educational research. This is one of the most progressive policy decisions ever made by a Ministry which, over the years, has rarely displayed an over-zealous enthusiasm for scientific method. It is the first stage in what ought to be, what must be, a chain reaction. Funds for research demand research workers. Expansion of research is impossible unless more researchers are trained. The implications for university departments and faculties of education are obvious, and need not, I trust, be stressed.

These three developments, I suggest, give us grounds for optimism, and for hoping for a rapid growth in our knowledge of the learning process. This, in turn, will lead to better training of better teachers, and a development in skills and techniques of teaching to exploit our new insights. The major challenge for the teacher and the educationist is to permit every child the full development of his talents. I am convinced that, at present, we fall very far below this utopian standard, and much further below than most teachers could possibly believe. By providing experiences and materials matching the pupil's stage of development, and taking into account his background and his potentialities, the so-called 'ceiling' to his possible performance and achievement is away beyond anything we at present envisage. We do not yet know all the answers, but what matters is that we have the will to discover these answers, and that we take care to use the best possible strategies in our quest for knowledge and for full professional competence.

Bibliography

ALLEN, E. A., 1963
Professional training of teachers: a review of research.
Educ. Res. 5. 200–215

BURT, C., 1955
The evidence for the concept of intelligence.
Brit. J. Educ. Psychol. 25. 158–177.

CASLER, L., 1961
Maternal deprivation: a critical review of the literature.
Monogr. Soc. Res. Child Devel. 26. 1–64

DE CHARMS, R. and MOELLER, G. H., 1962
Values expressed in American children's readers: 1800–1950.
J. Abnorm. Soc. Psychol. 64. 136–142

COGHILL, G. E., 1929
Anatomy and the problem of behaviour.
Camb: Camb. Univ. Press.

CRAWFORD, A. B., 1929
Incentives to Study.
New Haven: Yale Univ. Press.

DALE, R. R., 1952
Some non-academic factors influencing university students.
Brit. J. Sociol. 3. 14–19.

DENNIS, W., 1960
Causes of retardation among institutional children.
J. Genet. Psychol.

DERRICK, T., 1961
Social environment and success in the secondary school selection examination.
M. Ed. Thesis, Univ. of Manchester library.

EVANS, K. M., 1961
An annotated bibliography of British research on teaching
and teaching ability.
Educ. Res. 4. 67–80.

FLOUD, J. E., HALSEY, A. H., and MARTIN, F. M., 1957
Social class and educational opportunity.
Lond. Heinemann.

FOWLER, W., 1962
Cognitive learning in infancy and early childhood.
Psychol. Bull. 59. 116–52.

FRASER, E. D., 1959
Home environment and the school.
Lond: Lond. Univ. Press.

FURNEAUX, W. D., 1961
The chosen few.
Oxford Univ. Press.

GESELL, A and THOMPSON, H., 1929
Learning and growth in identical twin infants.
Genet. Psychol. Monogr. 6. 1–124.

GLIDEWELL, J. C. (Ed.) 1961
Parental attitudes and child behaviour.
Springfield, Ill. C. C. Thomas.

HARLOW, H. F., 1949
The formation of learning sets.
Psychol. Rev. 56. 51–65.

HEBB, D. O., 1949
The organisation of behaviour.
N. Y. John Wiley.

HIMMELWEIT, H. T., 1963
A social psychologist's view of the school psychological
service of the future.
Bull. Brit. Psychol. Soc. 16. 16–24.

HUNT, J. McV., 1961
Intelligence and experience.
N. Y. Ronald Press.

INHELDER, B., 1953
Criteria of the stages of mental development.

In: Tanner & Inhelder (Eds.). *Discussions on Child Development*, pp. 75–85.
N. Y. Int. Univ. Press.

ISMAIL, M. E., 1963
Relations between the parents' socio-economic level and their aspirations regarding their children's future.
Paper read at Int. Congr. of Psychol., Washington, D.C.

KUHLEN, R. G., 1963
Age and intelligence: the significance of cultural change in longitudinal v. cross-sectional findings.
Vita Humana. 6. 113–23.

LEIBOWITZ, H., 1961
Apparent visual size as a function of distance for mentally deficient subjects.
Amer. J. Psychol. 74. 98–100.

McGRAW, M. B., 1935
Growth: a study of Johnny and Jimmy.
N. Y. Appleton-Century-Crofts.

McKEACHIE, W. J., 1962
Procedures and techniques of teaching: a survey of experimental studies.
In: Sanford (Ed.) *The American College*, Chapt. 8.
N. Y., John Wiley.

McMAHON, D., 1962
The identification and use of talent.
Advanc. of Sci. 19. 322–29.

MURPHY, L. B., 1944
Childhood experiences in relation to personality.
In: Hunt (Ed.) *Personality and the behaviour disorders*, Chapt. 21.
N. Y. Ronald Press.

PIAGET, J., 1936
The origins of intelligence in children.
N. Y. Int. Univ. Press.

PIAGET, J., 1947
The psychology of intelligence.
Lond: Routledge & Kegan Paul.

PIDGEON, D. A., 1959
Educational guidance and standards of attainment.
Times Educ. Supp. 3rd Ap. 1959, p. 712.
RYANS, D. G., 1960
Characteristics of teachers.
Amer. Counc. on Educ., Washington, D.C.
SANFORD, N. (Ed.) 1962
The American College.
N. Y. John Wiley.
STERN, G. G., 1962
Environments for learning.
In: Sanford (Ed.) *The American College*, Chapt. 21.
N. Y., John Wiley.
SUCHMAN, J. R., 1960 a
Inquiry training and science education.
In: Rucklis (Ed.) *Laboratories in the classroom.*
N. Y. Science Materials Centre.
SUCHMAN, J. R., 1960 b
Inquiry training in the elementary school.
Sci. teacher 27. 42–47.
WISEMAN, S., 1959
Trends in educational psychology.
Brit. J. Educ. Psychol. 29. 128–135.
WISEMAN, S., 1962
Assessing the ability of experienced teachers.
Adv. of Sci. 20. 57–64.
WISEMAN, S., 1963
Characteristics of successful teachers.
Paper read to Int. Congr. Psychol., Washington, D.C.
WISEMAN, S., 1964
Education and environment.
Manchester: Manch. Univ. Press.
WOFINDEN, R. C., 1950
Problem families in Bristol.
Occas. Papers on Eugenics, 6. London: Cassell.

2

DORIS M. LEE

Perception, Intuition and Insight

The study of perception is the study of the way in which individuals gain the basic material for learning. Thus perceptual processes play a part in both initial and transitory stages of learning in a wide variety of fields. Hebb has pointed out that any response shown by an individual is also a stimulus for future development.[1] In this sense the processes of perception and learning are intermingled. It is, however, profitable to try to consider perception separately, because there is too often a tendency to assume that the necessary perceptual basis is present in any given learning situation. Perception is glossed over on the assumption that reasoning is of more importance. In their turn, intuition and insight may be treated as special aspects of the perceptual process.

Bartley has suggested that perception is the process by which an individual makes contact with the external world and with his fellows through the medium of his various senses.[2] This is a broad global definition of perception and offers no more than an indication of the scope of the field. It does, however, show some of the general characteristics of the process now to be looked at. Under the process of perception as described by Bartley, a person gradually builds up his own description of the external world. The process of percep-

[1] Hebb, D. O., *A Textbook of Psychology*, W. B. Saunders Co., 1958, p. 46.
[2] Bartley, S. H., *Principles of Perception*, N.Y. Harper Bros., 1958, p. 4.

42

tion thus has an individual basis. Each person builds his own idea of life as he experiences it, and his observations are certainly dependent on (*a*) his own capacities, and (*b*) the complexity of the perceptual field, which generally speaking lies within his normal surroundings. For any group of people there will of course be much overlap between their individual perceptions experienced within a common situation. One of the things we seek in teaching is to strengthen this overlap for certain selected groups of perceptions. Bartlett has pointed out that there will also be many individual variations.[1] Sometimes in teaching these variations are overlooked at the expense of strengthening the so-called overlap, but they do represent a large problem in human communication. In this connection it is perhaps worth while to remind ourselves that language provides the only overt demonstration of either overlap or individual variation. Hence, from the start, language assumes an important role in both perception and learning.

Before reviewing some of the results from the vast field of psychological work on perception and their importance for education, it might be worth while to look a little more closely at the nature of the process itself. The original archetype for the experimental study of human behaviour was the Stimulus-Response (SR) formula, and this simple formula was the basis of the study of human perception for many years, it being acknowledged that the action of the central nervous system was the physiological means of supplying the connection between the two aspects. Hebb has suggested a more rigorous analysis of the perceptual process as consisting of four stages; stimulus, sensation, perception and response.[2] First, every individual experiences a variety of stimuli all the time from his environment, his fellows, and his thoughts and ideas. Second, such stimuli produce sensations in the individual concerned. These sensations are plainly the results of

[1] Bartlett, Sir Frederick C., *Remembering*, Cambridge University Press, 1932, Introduction.
[2] Hebb, D. O., loc. cit., Chapter 9.

processes in the central nervous system and the brain, and may not rise beyond the quality of feelings. It is important to isolate this stage, since in some learning situations such unexpressed feelings are important, for example in the field of art or music appreciation, also in the field of perception of persons. Third, in most cases of stimulus followed by sensation, some reorganization of the reactions experienced takes place, and there is some internal registering by the individual of an event which has occurred. This stage Hebb classes as perception. Further, Hebb calls these reorganization processes 'mediating processes', since this does involve both a sorting of perceptual experiences and a placing of these into perspective against the individual's background of experience. Fourth, when the results of the perception are made plain by the individual concerned, either through the medium of language or gesture, a response has been overtly shown. Such responses represent only a small percentage of the stimuli and sensations, and not all of the perceptions experienced by the individual concerned.

This analysis of the broad process of perception into four stages is artificial in the sense that all four stages are accomplished consecutively in a very brief span of time. On the other hand, it seems of considerable importance for education in demonstrating the various points at which perceptual experiences may be arrested. In this sense it reflects the right of any individual to express, or to refrain from expressing, his reactions as he thinks appropriate. Furthermore it stresses once again the individuality of the perceptual process so far as group learning is concerned. It might be well to note that the production of a response does not in itself guarantee meaning. Meaning is largely gained by the active comparison of a particular response with past experience.

One further part of Hebb's theory sheds still further light on this question of perception. In classifying factors of behavioural development of all kinds, Hebb has suggested that we should differentiate between factors which he classes as 'sensory constant' and those which he classes as 'sensory variable'.[1] In this sense, he draws attention to the wide variety of stimuli which are normally inevitable for all human beings growing up in the same environment, as against the equally wide variety of stimuli which are a matter of individual background and individual opportunity for perceptual development. This again has wide implications for education, more particularly perhaps in relation to young children coming into the common environment of the school for the first time, but certainly also throughout the whole range of full-time education, and beyond that into the voluntary learning situations of adult life. M. D. Vernon again stresses this difference when she states that perceptual development depends essentially on exposure to the patterned stimulation of suitable environment.[2] This question of suitable environment is more of a problem today than ever before, either because of, or even despite, the levels of material prosperity.

At this point it might be appropriate to tie in to this discussion some further consideration of what is meant by intuition and insight. Common usage of these words tends to be rather like the assertion that 'Mr. X is a good teacher'— something of which the meaning is known by everyone, but no one can offer a working definition. It is extremely important to establish a more coherent perspective on intuition and insight, since the occurrence of the corresponding processes in individual persons is by no means rare. Such writing as is available tends to point to the likelihood that intuition and insight may be regarded as sensations and perceptions of a particular quality, rather than as separate processes in their own right.

Present-day writers in psychology tend to omit any discussion of intuition in treating either perception or learning —this province seems to be assigned to the philosophers. Presumably the study of intuition is peculiarly one of intro-

[1] Hebb, D. O., loc. cit., Chapter 6.
[2] Vernon, M. D., *The Psychology of Perception*, Penguin Books Ltd., 1962, p. 29 et seq.

spection only, and will remain so. In this sense it provides a constant reminder of the wide range of psycho-philosophical topics essential to the all-round study of human behaviour. For present purposes, it is suggested that intuition is best viewed as a form of sensation guiding an individual towards a perception and response highly appropriate to the situation under consideration, but not always completely explainable to an external observer. In this I am closely following Russell's notion that mathematical intuition is a feeling analogous to common sense, as to the sort of way a problem is likely to turn out.[1] I am also reflecting the description often given by an individual in the ordinary appraisal of behaviour under the word 'hunch'. Moreover, if sensations or feelings classed as intuition are those which either would or do actually lead to the best possible response, then intuition might be said to carry an element of unfulfilled foresight.

This element of unfulfilled foresight might well transform early intuition into later insight, for insight can be regarded as a special quality of perception. In Hebb's sequence of stimulus, sensation, perception and response, there are occasions in which the stage of perception—that is, the use of mediating processes to restructure the elements of the perceptual situation—is rapid, direct and productive of a highly effective solution. Hebb has commented that a problem solved by insight is one in which a direct solution appears with little previous warning. Frequently the use of insight follows the use of trial and error methods, but it must be recognized as a category very different from the slow perfecting of this type of learning in the more usual sense.

Broadbent, in his excellent book *Behaviour*, has summarized the evidence on the nature of insight stemming on the one hand from the work of Köhler in the Gestalt school, and from that of Hull in the behaviourist school on the other.[2] Over

---

[1] Russell, B., *Introduction to Mathematical Philosophy*, George Allen and Unwin Ltd., 1919, p. 145.

[2] Broadbent, D. E., *Behaviour*, Eyre and Spottiswoode Ltd., 1961, Chapter 4.

twenty years the consensus of this work would seem to indicate that the ability to exercise insight is partly innate (in that the brain can only form and accept perceptual patterns within its own limitations), and partly acquired (in that the restructuring of any perceptual situation is very much dependent on both the adequacy of previous experiences and on the recombination of these). In these aspects insight clearly has some parallels with intelligence.

Peel has asked whether insight can be developed.[1] Whilst this seems somewhat doubtful, it is immediately clear that optimum working conditions can allow for the proper emergence of insight in any given situation. In other words, while it would, in the face of the evidence, be unsafe to assume that insight can be developed, it certainly can be inhibited. Such is all too frequently the case in teaching, where insufficient use is made of the children's own perceptions, where the presentation of material is confused or skimpy, or where insightful solutions do not correspond to working methods. At the age of seven years, it transpired that my niece possessed some capacity for arithmetical insight, since evidently she began to use in school certain methods of calculation which she had picked up casually from her father at home. My brother received a letter from the school requesting him not to teach his daughter methods which they could not follow, but to teach her the ordinary school methods! My niece, however, refused to discard what she considered to be quick and suitable methods, and it took a great deal of tact to smooth the situation down. It is particularly true in mathematics that insightful solutions tend not to correspond with the more straightforward methods of work. The same is true of certain aspects of work in other subjects, though insight is frequently a more welcome characteristic. Perhaps this apparent lack of correspondence between insightful and more orthodox perceptions caused Peel to suggest that insight might be developed by verbalizing the work as it proceeds,

[1] Peel, E. A., *The Psychological Basis of Education*, Oliver and Boyd, 1958, pp. 55–62.

though again this might simply be a question of clarifying the situation so that the emergence of insight is both possible and worthwhile.[1]

It is time now to turn for a few minutes to some of the results obtained in formal experiments in perception, and particularly to examine something of their relevance to normal learning situations. In education we are entirely concerned with complex situations, but much of the experimental work has been done in much simpler conditions under laboratory control. This offers no reason for discounting the results of the latter work. We must seek what help we can from it to throw light on the former, at the same time attempting to mount corresponding investigations into the nature of perception in more complex situations.

The oldest and most thorough field of work in perception was carried out within the Gestalt school of Psychology in the early part of this century under the leadership of Wertheimer, Koffka and Köhler. This was entirely concerned with the analysis of behaviour in simple perceptual situations. The main emphasis was on *what* is perceived, and the results offered some useful indications for understanding the perceptual process in more complex situations. The main outcomes of the Gestalt school were:

(1) The perceiver himself organizes his field into *figure* and *ground*. The figure then commands the whole attention of the perceiver, and the ground receives little or no further consideration.

(2) It follows that the perceiver organizes his own pattern from the perceptual field presented to him. This may or may not be the pattern intended from him. The Gestalt workers thought that this organization was independent of previous learning but later work has negated this idea.

(3) The perceiver tends to look for simplicity, regularity and completeness. Simpler perceptions take precedence over more complex ones.

(4) There is a tendency to perceive incomplete material as

[1] Peel, E. A., loc. cit., p. 61.

complete. This led Köhler to offer a definition of insight as a set of processes supplying the most appropriate final link in a situation presented as incomplete, again corroborating the view that insight is to be regarded as a quality of perception. This also led to the fashionable use of the phrase 'flash of insight'.

(5) The perceiver works within a frame of reference mainly constituted by his former experience, and this gives final interpretation and meaning to his acknowledged response.

These main results from the Gestalt school have strong implications for (*a*) the classroom learning situation, (*b*) the field of visual aids in particular, and (*c*) the more general and less organized perceptual situations. It may be that they are now inherent in every teaching situation, but it seems possible that more use could be made of them, especially at the secondary level. The results suggest in the first place that the expected perceptions from any situation, classroom or general, be viewed entirely from the angle of the perceiver. Secondly, they indicate firm consideration of the structure of such learning situations to ensure the maximum likelihood that the desired perceptions will be made by the perceivers, and moreover that no ambiguity will be introduced by the perceiver looking for regularity, balance or symmetry. Lastly some attention should be paid to the fact that closure will operate whether or not it is in the right direction. In the latter context care should be taken to give sufficient direction where a particular goal is desirable. In mathematical and scientific subjects, the end-point in any perceptual process is uniquely determined. In most arts subjects, or in more general situations, this is not the case, and the perceiver can very easily use his ability for closure to jump to the wrong conclusions, unless firm direction is inherent in the perceptual situation itself. Lastly, in classroom perception in particular, the well-known essential provision of common background experience has long been recognized as important, but is not always sufficiently evaluated in direct relation to its purpose.

Visual aids represent an important special field in relation to the Gestalt theory of perception. One of the main functions of any visual aid is to set in train the right kind and quantity of perceptions from which learning can take place. The other function is, of course, to contribute equally to the development of the learning processes based on these perceptions. The same considerations as were applied to teaching situations should be applied in evaluating any visual aid. Too often these fail from a lack of attention to the right kind of features in favour of using those alternative features which make for a more acceptable and attractive whole.

In more general fields of learning outside the classroom, particularly in aspects of social and community learning, perceptual situations are less clear-cut, and the possible responses coloured by rather less controllable external factors. Indeed, it is usually impossible to present perceptual situations; invariably it is necessary to appraise a situation as it is, and in this context the background of experience and the personal qualities of the perceiver will have a strong effect on his perceptual organization of the situation. Unhappily, when teenagers and adults are presented with structured situations in ordinary life, there is too often a misleading twist to the structure which will cause certain perceptual responses at the expense of others, unless the perceiver exercises the greatest caution. In advertising, for example, the outstanding characteristics tend to be for attraction, and particularly in teenage levels, tend to be for attraction at the expense of other considerations. In political propaganda, especially before general elections, presentation of data in the form of charts is frequently distorted according to party preferences for the kind of perceptions likely to be made. Too much manœuvre in personal and professional life is a matter of stressing some elements in a group situation so that certain consequences or courses of action are inevitable. A fine line operates between the utilization of perceptual responses to further the individual's understanding of himself, his environment, and other people, and the erroneous utilization of these same perceptual processes to sway his emotions and his intellect along directions which may be more fruitful to other people than to himself. These rather negative considerations certainly have relation to the topics covered by the last five contributions to this book.

Returning now to development in the psychology of perception, later work has developed in several directions—perception of particular elements such as shape, size, distance and colour either singly or in combination, the kinds of perception to be expected at the different stages of child development, factors affecting perception, and work on personality characteristics in relation to the perceptual process. The particularized experiments on single elements, such as perception of distance, have broadened the Gestalt principles over certain narrow fields. One significant development of this work has led to attempts to differentiate between the relative effects of shape and colour on individual perception. All the evidence points to a predominant influence of shape at every level above the age of entry into school.[1] This suggestion that shape is the more readily perceived indicates that the indiscriminate use of colour in educational products might be reconsidered in relation to its perceptual value. Apparently colour makes for pleasantness rather than accurate perception.

Side by side with the more detailed work on the perception of shape, size, distance and colour have been studies in child development which suggest the kind of perceptions which seem to be normal for children at different levels of chronological age. The work of Gesell, M. M. Lewis and Isaacs all concur with the well-known structure of perceptual development outlined by Piaget within the broad age categories of birth-2, 2–4, 4–7, 7–11, 11–14 years, the development of the perceptual responses themselves being closely tied to language development. The transition in quality through the age-ranges is one from disjointed unco-ordinated responses in the early years through to smoothly co-ordinated responses

[1] Vernon, M. D., loc. cit., Chapter 6.

in reasonably complex situations in the later years. This kind of transition is, of course, also mirrored in the corresponding growth of conceptual thought.

One very important development of this work on the perception of different elements, whether related to the nature or quality of the perceptions entailed, has been M. D. Vernon's investigation into the perception of different kinds of complex material.[1] This work has been carried out with children of school age and with adults. The material studied has comprised pictures, the printed word, and charts and diagrams. The general results suggest that for ease of perception, pictures come before the printed word, and the latter before charts and diagrams. Much work on perception has been carried out in relation to learning to read, and this has had widespread influence in schools; it is neither desirable nor necessary to review this here. Much less thought has been given to the perception of pictures, charts, or diagrams. M. D. Vernon suggests that pictures form a two-dimensional representation of a three-dimensional reality, and that the perceiver has to develop a capacity to utilize picture material symbolically to suggest the associated concepts and ideas from real life. She further asserts: 'But this capacity must be learned, and the child acquires it only gradually, and sometimes only after much teaching.'[2] A stern reminder that the capacity to acquire information from pictures is too frequently taken for granted.

The casual supposition that pictures are easily perceived and receive accurate interpretation is no doubt enhanced in this country by their very ready provision in the child's background right from his early years. When visiting African schools in Southern Rhodesia, the writer took the opportunity to experiment with some very simple pictures in that setting. The results threw into sharp relief the notion that children have to be taught to recognize the representation shown in a picture as well as to abstract information

[1] Vernon, M. D., loc. cit., p. 112 et seq.
[2] Vernon, M. D., loc. cit., p. 102.

from it. At that time there was no provision of pictures in the African child's background which in any way began to be comparable to the multitudinous ways that are everyday occurrences here. In most schools just the one regulation set of wall pictures was available and could be perceived accurately, presumably because of long practice by teacher and pupils. But the introduction of new pictures of very simple and well-known features, such as local huts or fruits, led to no response without a good deal of discussion, and clearly were not easily absorbed by the children concerned. This study highlighted both the powerful effect of background and the need for training in the perception of two-dimensional picture material representing three-dimensional objects.

Looking now at the perception of charts and diagrams, this shows a further relevance of perceptual training. Children whose ages ranged between ten and fourteen years made very poor scores on work requiring this kind of perception, but after ten minutes of instruction their scores were much improved. Grammar school pupils and adults were able to perceive the actual information, but were unable to interpret the charts and diagrams without further help. These comparable studies of the perception of pictures, charts and diagrams highlight the unevenness of individual perception of different kinds of material, as well as the need for training in accurate perception. Such training needs to be fostered and encouraged at all stages of education starting from the lowest level.

General influences of perceptual studies on the curriculum have been most readily evident to teachers of young children. Infant teachers, probably because of the very nature of their task, have long been aware of the kind of perceptions made by their pupils, and are adept at using these in the interests of each individual child. Junior teachers have become more aware of the need to examine, utilize and develop children's perceptions in encouraging their more formal work. Secondary teachers have been the slowest to investigate the nature of the perceptions made by the people they teach. No doubt seniority of age brings more sophistication to the perceptual process and more of a common background within any working group, but individual differences and difficulties are still present.

Much consideration needs to be given to questions of perception at the secondary stage, where the field of school learning is formally divided into subjects. Not only does the necessary amount of training in perception differ between the subjects, but the kind of perceptions required and the kind of senses brought into play, may differ as well. Little evidence other than 'hunch by experience' is available here. It is clear that mathematicians and scientists, in particular, should stop relying on the precision of their material to ensure that the correct perceptions are made by their pupils, and recognize that careful training in perception is part of their task. It might even be possible that differences between girls' and boys' achievements in verbal and mathematical subjects would disappear if more attention were paid to the kind of perceptual responses asked and received; this is certainly a matter for serious examination. It may be that different perceptual training is necessary for boys and girls in both the verbal and non-verbal fields. It may also be that an insufficient use is made of senses other than the visual-auditory set. The psychological work, as it stands, merely points to the need for careful examination of the perceptual responses expected and received in each of the subjects normally represented in the secondary school curriculum; it offers no ready-made solution.

One new intervention in the educational field which may throw light on this question of perception is the introduction of programmed learning, a technique which relies very heavily on the capacity for visual perception, and the likelihood that each pupil will make the same (expected) perceptions from the one piece of proffered material. The latter might well not be the case. Evaluation of this kind of point will be critical to the right use of programmed learning techniques. It will also further elucidate some of the problems of the perceptual process itself.

Perhaps it is appropriate to consider at this point something of the general factors affecting perception, most of which can be bipolar in their effects on the perceptual process. Hebb's analysis of this process into stimulus-sensation-perception-response suggests three main categories of factors known to play a part. These are physiological needs and pressures, environmental effects, and characteristics within the individual. These cover all the factors well-known to teachers such as clarity of presentation, including intensity and manner of application of stimuli; relevance to past experience and present purpose; motivation, attitude, interest, attention; intelligence, achievement, mood, physical health of the perceiver. Of these, the relevant psychological work is chiefly concerned with general motivation, past experience and attention.

Motivation is a somewhat obscure concept embracing all those factors which make or mar activity within the perceiver. That these factors are important is clear, but exactly what they are is somewhat difficult to tell, since information can only be gleaned from an analysis of observations of the perceptual situation on the one hand and of the comments of the perceiver on the other. Any assessment of motivation is bound to be subjective, but two things are clear. First, there is a profile of motivational factors operating in any situation, and the outcome is affected by the particular combination of these factors. Second, this profile probably differs considerably from one individual to another, even within the same group. This profile of motivational factors is no doubt the biggest determinant in the individual's selectivity amongst the possible stimuli in the perceptual field, and always includes the factors of past experience and attention.

In this context, past experience is clearly one of the main factors in forming the individual's expectation of a new situation, and includes in its orbit rather more than previous knowledge. Emotional overtones provide one of the less

55

desirable offshoots here. Adequate training can override its effects, but this tends to be a long-term policy. Past experience also contributes to the preperceptual attitudes shown by the perceiver, and thus to what is known as sets or determinants of perception. Observations of patients whose sight or hearing has been restored by operation provide excellent indications of the part played by past experience in visual and auditory perception by revealing the difficulties when such experience is not present, and demonstrate how much is taken for granted in the normal field.

Studies of attention have usually been carried out in the more simplified laboratory situations where other external factors are more easily controlled. Three points arising out of this work might be raised here. Where it is permitted at all, direction of attention should be as good as possible. Instructions and other forms of teaching are particularly important. Clarity and directness are desirable. Second, different types of attention are relevant to different types of perceptual situation, for instance calm and lengthy consideration may sometimes be preferable to the highly concentrated attention preceding a snap decision. Particular individuals may not possess the capacity for the type of attention needed in a given situation. Third, the span of attention is certainly limited as regards assimilation of content, and the all-over amount attended to at any one time tends to be constant. Thus if too many details are required, attention is diffused. If a few details only are to be attended to, attention is focused on these. If the opportunity to structure a perceptual situation is possible, account may be taken of this constancy of attention. In more general everyday life situations, where such structure may not be possible, the amount of detail attended to will be influenced by the characteristics of the situation and the personality of the perceiver.

The final question to touch on briefly is a rather more theoretical one. Attempts have been made to establish perceptual types, the assumption being that any one person approaches all perceptual situations in the same manner.

Effort has also been made to relate these so-called perceptual types to some of the main personality characteristics. Klein, Witkin, Gardner, Bartlett and Thurstone have led the work in this field. The work on perceptual types has suggested a possible dichotomy of synthetic (those persons who view the perceptual field as an integrated whole) as against analytic (those persons who concentrate more on the separate sections, or on detail), or the more well-known objective-subjective groupings. The consensus of this work appears to be towards an approach to perception dictated by characteristics within the individual and not by the situation to be perceived. But M. D. Vernon has shown that certain kinds of more precise perceptions are a matter of training, and therefore the related perceptual approach can be acquired, whatever the individual's previous perceptual pattern. Hence one cannot expect, in practice, to find more or less definite perceptual types, but only some bias towards one perceptual approach.

Attempts to relate perceptual types to certain personality traits have as yet yielded little success, probably due to the intrinsic difficulties in separating off the effects of personality factors from all other factors affecting perception. It is clear, however, that broad personality profiles such as are embodied in the introvert-extrovert classification have some relation to the ways in which individuals tend to perceive. Moreover, there is some evidence that the value system of the individual, as measured by (say) the Allport-Vernon-Lindsey Study of Values, has some relation to what is likely to be perceived in both individual and group situations. Little work has been done, as yet, to extend this work to person-to-person perceptions, though one of my own students, Mr. El-Meligi, has recently collected some interesting evidence which suggests that values tend to affect the individual's perceptions of others in a group where the members were reasonably well known to each other.[1] This work on the relation of personality characteristics to perception is still in

[1] El-Meligi, M. H. A. A., *M.A. Thesis*, University of London, 1963.

its early stages, and it would be unsafe to place too much emphasis on any of the evidence. On the other hand, such work is important in interpersonal perception, and it is imperative to continue the search for new and better techniques in this field.

These few remarks about perceptual types and their relation to personality characteristics complete the survey of existing fields of work on perception and their relation to the educative processes. There are many gaps in this work which require to be further explored. Some of the important issues requiring attention are as follows. All stem from a consideration of the perceptual process as it operates in the two broad categories of classroom and more general learning situations. In the University of Amsterdam Institute of Education opportunity has been afforded for observers to keep accurate accounts of series of lessons in the Dutch language and arithmetic. Three parallel first-year classes are each being taught through a different approach in each subject. The verbatim account of the lessons together with recording of pupil reactions and behaviour is enabling much light to be thrown on the nature of perception in the customary teaching situation, as well as in relation to the teaching approaches themselves. Such a process looks at the pupil's perceptions both in their own right and in comparison to the ones expected by the teacher. It pinpoints the variety of responses evoked by one stimulus, though it leaves untouched the questions of the variety of stimuli which could lead to the same response. It allows of some evaluation of the factors which appear to be controlling perception in that situation, especially in relation to the different methods of teaching. This research in Amsterdam has made a beginning in a much needed field of perceptual research.

More of this work is needed. We could all offer rough check answers to the three points raised, but objective and controlled assessment may well give different results. Some preliminary studies by Hughes indicate that the perceptions of many children in the classroom are very different from what adults commonly assume them to be.[1] More particularly some preliminary work of my own in arithmetic demonstrated that in a group of seven-year-old children there were very different perceptions of one simple number process, leading to a variety of ways of working, though one method had been taught. More generally, anyone who has taken part in Kim's game has seen the variety of perceptual patterns which can be formed from one tray of objects shown for the same length of time to one group of people. Many similar examples could be quoted on the number of related responses possible from a single stimulus and vice-versa. These are practical considerations in the teaching situation which are not always dealt with adequately for the individual person. Often in teaching, overt responses are ignored if they are not just what is required, but this provides no help for the individual giving the response and may well cause frustration or other inhibitions. Viewed on a wider scale, more information about and understanding of the ranges of possible stimuli and responses would enable happier adjustments in both general and specific learning situations. Lastly, much more information is needed on factors affecting perception, and concentrated effort on this would yield dividends in understanding a variety of facets in human behaviour. Such information requires a more clinical approach than that offered by attitude scale or questionnaire techniques. In particular, it is desirable to obtain more evidence on redundancy of information, a state in which we may place the growing child inadvertently at any stage of his development, and one which affects equally his responses and his inclination to continue further. The results of such studies might well cut to a minimum the waste of time and energy involved in many school and life situations.

[1] Hughes, M. M., *Development of the Means for the Assessment of the Quality of Teaching in Elementary Schools*. Salt Lake City, Utah: University of Utah, 1959.

3

W. D. WALL

Learning to Think

My aim in this talk is to attempt to bring about some relationship between learning theory and educational practice. We shall be particularly concerned with the classroom context, with the way in which children develop and how their environment may contribute to or inhibit clear, effective types of thinking.

I should make it quite clear that I am not going to talk about all forms of mental activity. Reverie and fantasy, for example, are forms of mental activity but not necessarily forms of effective thinking. I am going to concern myself with those specific aspects of thinking which are by and large disciplined: such, for example, as reasoning and problem solving, judgement (a somewhat vague concept, since it often means the end result of a process of thought rather than thought itself); and finally with so-called 'creative' thought —again whatever this may mean.

It seems true to say that disciplined, rational thinking is or should be a major, if not the major, objective of education. Rational thinking will be concerned with the solution of such practical problems as: will this shelf fit into this space? can I afford to buy this object? if I buy this object will I have more value for my money than if I buy that? Effective thinking of this kind will be one of the marks of a well-educated person. It will be concerned too with the solution of personal problems; with the formulation of judgements about people, about politics and morals. As such it will involve emotions and wishes as well as strictly rational elements. Thus one may say that in pursuit of the training of rational thought, an important educational object will be to teach people to distinguish from the strictly objective and rational elements, the emotional and irrational ones which are likely to influence judgement, problem-solving and even tend to determine the choice of problems to be solved and the selection of data to solve them. In addition it should equip us with the techniques for holding these at arm's length.

We can put this in a more concise way and define education as the process of acquiring independence in thought—independence in the sense that the rational process is in fact rational and not unconsciously warped by prejudice. It could indeed be argued that, from the time the child comes into the school to the time he leaves it, his education should be marked by the attainment of a series of increasingly complex intellectual independences. We know for example that the young child passes, given adequate experience, with a certain amount of ease from percepts to concepts. We know that the general trend of development is from the concrete to the abstract and that one of the businesses of education is to equip the child with the symbolisms—verbal, numerical, mathematical, musical and so on—which enable him to manipulate abstract thought. Another objective of education might well be stated as that of fostering a move from an absolute rule (whether in arithmetic, the rules of a game, or moral judgement) to the acceptance of the fact that rules are relative and can be modified in the light of circumstances. Education, too, is I suppose in part at any rate, concerned with the change from emotionally dominated and intuitive (i.e., dependent and partial) to more objective (i.e., independent and rational) thought.

At this point we might turn these apparently confident statements into questions and ask ourselves whether in fact these results come about, and if they do, whether this is brought about by education or is simply the consequence of growth and maturation. Piaget and many others have shown us that there appear to be genetic sequences in the thinking of children away, for example, from the sensory and concrete and therefore specific and rigid to more generalized and therefore more flexible types of thinking. However, all along the line there is a triple danger. First, a child may move away from, shall we say, perceptual types of rigidity but in doing so he may develop new kinds of rigidities—for example, the tendency to apply a method of thought or problem solving, blindly; or worse still, he may apply learned solutions regardless of their applicability. At the adult level this is to become the victim of one's experience; in other terms, to fight the war before last. A learned solution is used in inapplicable circumstances and is therefore a wrong and even dangerous one. The second danger is that in teaching—or helping children to learn to think—we may set up interferences by inducing failure and negative emotions, by arousing anxiety and insecurity. This is most clearly seen in what happens in the teaching of arithmetic which is a formal, logical and abstract process with a clearly right and wrong answer. Premature teaching and especially premature abstraction can be severely damaging. But the danger is not confined to arithmetic. It can occur in any aspect of the curriculum, in any educative event of a child's life—wherever in fact he is confronted with demands, expectations and choices he is not mature enough to meet.

The third danger is one of which most of us are unaware but which is pervasive and, in my view, particularly damaging to the intellectually able. In order to help children and adolescents to learn to think, we have, of course, to give them ideas and facts to think about as well as techniques appropriate to the manipulation of ideas and facts; that is to say we tend to have 'subjects', organized bodies of knowledge, a definable curriculum. We teach mathematics, physics, history, literature and so on. Thinking and problem solving tend, therefore, to be exercised in relation to specific classes of items of experience. Each area of study has effective strategies of problem solving, types of thinking and so on which are, in part, peculiar to it. One cannot imagine a solely arithmetical technique appropriate to literary understanding. On the other hand, judgement in any field involves, among other things, the definition and delimitation of the problem to be solved, the marshalling of evidence, the determination of its relevance, the setting up of a trial solution and its testing in as objective a way as possible. In teaching subjects—particularly when these are being prepared for examinations—there is a strong and natural tendency to teach them for their own sake, and not to perceive that if generalization of problem solving strategies is to take place, it must be brought about deliberately. There is a good deal of evidence to suggest that one cannot train 'faculties' by 'disciplines' and that the transfer of training is only of limited automatic occurrence. It is more than open to surmise that if the general elements of problem solving are made apparent to the pupil and if he is taught to apply scientific or mathematical or formally logical forms of reasoning outside the narrow bounds of the subject in which he first learned them, real transfer will take place. One must in short systematically and consciously teach for transfer: otherwise the very effectiveness of our teaching of the specific strategies applicable to the problems of a specific discipline may act as a block to effective thought in many other areas. In illustration, one may remark how frequent it is that scientists fail to apply scientific rigour to emotionally charged problems outside their science and how many 'well-educated' people in public and private life are quite incapable of developing problem-solving strategies to meet new problems, but rely upon learned responses whose appropriateness they do not even question.

At this point, perhaps, we might try provisionally to define the dimensions of a problem situation. A problem is perceived as such when the progress to a goal by an obvious route is impossible and when an automatism does not provide an effective answer. At this point one may do one of two things: one may refuse to see that the problem exists, an emotional denial which happens more often than we think, perhaps particularly in committees concerned with education; or one may accept that a problem exists and attempt to define what it is by asking a number of questions aimed to understand the propositions that delimit it.

The next stage is to look at the data at disposal and to discriminate those parts of them which are likely to be relevant, to perceive the gaps and, if possible, to fill them with further relevant information. These processes are in one substantial sense imaginative and creative; but a series of even more imaginative and creative processes follows—those of formulating trial hypotheses, of making a selection (if you have them) among learned responses, of developing new responses or of recombining old ones. By and large this will be true, whether you are a child solving a conventional problem in arithmetic or whether you are an adult confronted with a problem in your private life. When some hypotheses and some methods have been formulated, you try them out, you check them; and finally comes the process of evaluation or judgement.

This sketchy analysis makes clear that in the teaching situation (as well as in the ordinary human one) there are a number of qualifying statements which we ought to make. First of all, the person concerned with a problem must perceive—must be *motivated* to perceive—that the problem exists and he must want to solve it. If he doesn't want to solve the problem, he may not even want to see it and of course a good deal of teaching teaches children that the best thing to do is not to see that a problem exists. Second, it is quite clear that in any problem, even the most elementary, the solver will need to possess or to find relevant items of knowledge. Some of these will derive from his previous learnings and his previous problem solvings; some he may have to search for. Here let me again state the obvious: that a problem for which no data exist cannot be solved; it probably will not even be seen as a problem. This was true, for example, about the 'flatness' of the earth; it was true about things like the circulation of the blood. Until certain kinds of information be-

64

came available in the environment, neither of these was perceived as a problem and no solution could be sought. Thirdly,
the solver will need to be master of a good many techniques.
For example, if it is a mathematical problem he will need to
know how to multiply; if he is going to paint, he will need to
know how to mix and apply the paint; and so on. He will
need strategies for formulating and testing his hypotheses and
he will need some criteria of judgement—probably some
form of measurement. These considerations and needs will
apply in different ways either at the most abstract level of
thinking or in strictly concrete and manipulatory terms.

A little while ago I was watching my very young child—he
was about ten months old at the time—playing with the
problem of how to open a cupboard door. The door had a
little bolt on it which was fairly loose: and this presented him
with a series of problems. First of all he pulled the knob on
the bolt towards him. When this didn't work, he rattled it
and found that by sliding it to the side he could pull open the
door. When he wanted to try again, he found that pushing
the door back with the bar pushed did not permit him to
shut the door. The problem he was seeking did not reappear;
there was another in its place. For a long time he played
around with this and eventually found out the highly complicated sequence of pulling the bolt back when you'd got
the door open and keeping it back if you wanted to shut it.
He then went on to repeat this many times, practised it, and
sorted it out. This was partly a trial and error type of response
and partly highly insightful reasoning. This example illustrates two things; what I have just been trying to state as the
dimensions of problem solving; but something much more
important, that the problem solving activity of the young
child leads to *new* learning. Even at that level there were certain kinds of techniques which he acquired and which presumably will make him a menace with any other cupboard in
the future. This element of spontaneous acquisition of new
techniques and the discovery of new problems is often what
is lacking in conventional teaching.

There are many techniques which mankind has developed —diagrammatic representation, verbal symbolism, mathematical and other symbolic languages—as tools for problem solving. We cannot sensibly expect children to discover these for themselves. Hence we have to think in terms of providing circumstances for children in a variety of ways which, as it were, frame the problem-solving activity. We can also notice from the example which I have just given, that trial and error behaviour is characteristic very often of animals, and often of young children. Such behaviour nearly always occurs, even in adults, when the problem cannot be conceptualized. If blind trial and error works, it will with repetition lead to some sort of conditioned response, i.e., learning without insight which may become rigid. If, on the other hand, the trial and error gives way to insight then it will lead to short-cutting which may or may not lead in its turn to a straight conditioned response but at least will give the possibility of transfer and generalization. In terms of learning a specific response, both of these seem to be fairly effective. However, trial and error followed by practice, though fairly effective, is not in all cases either the most economical or educationally, probably, the most desirable way. Moreover if the problem is difficult or impossible to conceptualize and nevertheless the motivations or incentives to solve it are very strong, it may produce a panic type of trial and error—a panic type of reaction—which may in its turn lead either to inhibition, to avoidance, to loss of interest, to countermotivation, or finally to refusal. This is the sort of thing that you see very often with children who have repeatedly failed in arithmetic.

The educational problem then is not that of avoiding trial and error learning altogether, but of recognizing that it easily degenerates into panic and blockage; and that anyway it may produce an undesirable rigidity in learned responses. What we wish to secure is a situation which permits insight and, through insight, generalization and transfer.

These rather scattered points have a considerable bearing

upon the construction of curricula and upon the methods which we use. The first concerns content. To solve almost any problem you need a certain amount of information. There is thus a strong case for the straight learning of facts, relationships, techniques. You cannot dispense with the counters of thinking. Some of these will be provided by the experience given by the child's own environment but many more could be acquired in the course of problem solving and thinking. Here, however, there is a word of warning: for the teacher, knowledge is the result of long past problems and learning and thinking. For the child, the acquisition of knowledge may in fact be either the authoritarian memorizing type of process which equips him with certain facts, solutions and overlearned techniques, but does not necessarily help him to understand the processes underlying them; or, on the other hand, it may be, if it is properly handled, itself a process of thinking. It seems probable that ordinary teaching may, with very similar content, either stimulate the process of thinking itself—the problem-solving which underlies the relationships of facts—avoid, or even deaden it.

How far the problem solving is stimulated or avoided depends on the teacher's own views about how important this is and how important are the relationships involved; but it also depends upon whether the child is or is not mature enough to accept it and to carry through the reasoning processes involved. For example, in teaching a child fractions it may well be found that with certain children at certain stages, it is simpler and more effective to tell them to turn upside down and multiply and encourage them to apply this as a blind technique in the solving of other problems than it would be to get them to understand why you turn upside down and multiply. I am not prepared either to attack or defend this as a procedure. It is possible, and I think all of us in our own educational experience have found this, to learn certain things first in a more or less mechanical way and later only, to develop an understanding of the reasons and principles which underlie them. The danger inherent in this is that it tends to produce a rigid type of response because the child does not understand it. Thus, if for any reason it is necessary to teach in a more or less authoritarian way techniques or facts, then one should also make a mental note to bring about understanding of the principles involved at some later stage.

So much, then, rather sketchily, for the content. More important, I think, is the question of method. Children have to be trained, just as adults do, how to approach and tackle problems. There are certain general notions here as to what should be taught: getting the questions right; making sure that the right question to define the kind of problem is asked; seeking out the relevant data; setting up the kind of hypothesis that can be tested as distinct from the kind of hypothesis which is an untestable noise; the trial or experiment; and the evaluation. These things need to be explicit and are of general bearing; but there are certain other aspects specific to the kind of problem with which the child is confronted. For example, problems involving multiplication or division are quite different from those involving the finding of means to express unique experiences in words, in colour or in line.

These are matched by a third consideration which conditions what is educationally possible and desirable. By and large one risks disaster if children are expected to undertake levels of thinking for which they are not ready. Piaget and others have taught us that there is a progression in the development of conceptualization and in the development of reasoning. An important stage along the road should have taken place before school; children should by five have passed from simple precepts to the preoperational handling of concepts. This however will not necessarily be true over the whole field of child thought, nor for all children. There will be important qualifications related particularly to the social group from which the children come and the kinds of experience their homes have provided. But basically the primary school teacher is concerned with the two stages which Piaget describes as 'intuitive thought' and 'concrete operations'.

68

At this point we may quickly refresh our memories of what Piaget calls intuitive thought. He means that intelligent behaviour is limited to overt action and thinking is tied very tightly to perceptual factors; there is no real reversibility and there is very little in the way of conservation. That is, the child can indicate absent objects by the use of signs but they are still concrete in his environment. He does not generalize. This means that real symbolization is for him somewhat abstract and remote. In the next stage, the actions of combining and dissociating, ordering, setting up correspondence, become grouped and are capable of deliberate reversal. This, if you like, is the stage at which the child can manipulate concretely almost anything in his environment but he is still concerned with actual operations on concrete objects. Though he can classify and serialize and can use numbers in a chanting kind of way, they are still very much tied to sensory perceptions, particularly, of course, things like counting and checking and what not. He needs to check his counting and serializing against real perceived models.

Piaget assigns fairly wide age-ranges to these: to the first 4–7; to the second 8–11 years. There is reason, I think, to suppose from some of the English work that these processes will be speeded or slowed according to the sorts of experience which the child gets but the evidence also suggests that the sequence is none the less fairly fixed, and that, if these sequences are transgressed, there is real danger of inducing kinds of rigidity of thinking which will inhibit learning later on.

The third stage concerns principally the teacher of adolescents. It is the full development of reasoned thinking, of capacity to handle propositional or formal operations. The child is capable of reasoning on a variety of relational factors, and able to accept a proposition 'as if it were true' and to reason from it. He has developed operational schemata and the genuine basis of abstract, logical and mathematical thought.

This is a development which does not universally or auto-

matically take place. Nor does it necessarily follow from ordinary educational experience. A great many people in fact do
not get beyond the concrete operational sort of stage though
they may appear to operate at more abstract levels because of
the way they verbalize. In determining whether or not pupils
will progress from the concrete operational to a higher stage, the
various languages acquired in or improved by education are
probably critical—particularly the mother tongue itself, and
the mathematical types of symbolism. In the light of this, we
may look again at pacing—at the idea of trying to match to
the course of a child's development, curriculum and method,
the kinds of problems which are put before him and the kinds
of strategies which he is helped to use. Two things become
immediately apparent: any content, method, or problem
which presupposes a stage in development not yet attained is
likely to lead the child to a trial and error type of behaviour,
and to rote memorizing. If the incentives to learn are
authoritarian and punitive, panic and avoidance tend to
become marked aspects of behaviour. This is very noticeable,
of course, in problems in learning arithmetic and mathematics. Even where the teaching is good and relations between teacher and taught are warm and friendly, premature
teaching may lead to the adoption of rigid strategies without
understanding and therefore incapable of generalization.
We see this quite often in the child who conforms well to a
reasonably humane school and becomes very good at doing
mechanical arithmetic but who gets progressively more and
more floored as his (more usually her) problems move away
from the kind which he or she has learned to solve. The
second risk is in some ways more serious. Highly authoritarian teaching may eventually provoke revolt. The accepting, pleasant teacher whom the children very much like
makes it difficult for them to let him down. If the environment, that is to say, the home and the school, does not
specifically foster the type of growth transition from one
state or level of thinking to the next, thus preparing a child
for further stages in the content of his curriculum, the growth

itself will be delayed and not merely in intellectual ways. One has the not unfamiliar picture of a child who is expected—because of success gained hitherto—to be ready for a further stage and who chronologically ought to be at that stage, but who in fact has become fixated in a form of success which does not allow for growth. They are like a sports player who has acquired a high degree of skill but whose very level of attainment inhibits the recombination and modification of that skill into more complex forms. This, I think, is peculiarly likely to happen to those children whose use of language (in Bernstein's formulation) is in fact largely of the 'public type', and who therefore lack the instrument with which steadily to make more and more precise the concepts with which they deal.

As children pass through the educational system, verbal conceptual development becomes increasingly important. It is the first and most flexible series of symbolisms available to thought. This is perhaps one of the reasons why many children who seem to be quite good and quite bright in the early primary years, tend to tail off towards the end of the primary school and decline markedly in the secondary school. Because their language is neither rich nor precise and because the school does not or cannot compensate for this, such children find increasing difficulty in formulating problems of the more complex and abstract type with which they are confronted. They are driven to attempt to reduce the abstract to concrete, manipulatory forms; and if this is impossible, the problem for them cannot be solved. Here, as an aside, we may point out the danger inherent in visual aids. Visual methods which make things simpler by making them more concrete, may tend, if they are not properly used, to fixate children at this stage. Educationally speaking, they are props only and should be deliberately used as *aids* to the formulation of problems in symbolic forms, particularly perhaps in the form of verbal symbolization. Otherwise the visual aid, while appearing to simplify the teaching task, may in fact contribute to inhibit subsequent development.

In the light of what has so far been said, I should like to consider some methods and to draw your attention to an excellent article, 'Teaching Problem Solving', by Williams in *Educational Research*. Williams takes the evidence for various methods of helping children to learn effective thinking and discusses this in the light of what can be done in the classroom. He points out, for example, that there is considerable evidence that with young children concrete presentation of problems is effective but that with adults and, particularly with intelligent adults, it is not as effective. This is what you would expect from the work of Piaget and others; that as the more effective tool of symbolization becomes dominant in thinking so the merely sensory (concrete) presentation of a problem in specific form is likely to be less efficient, less general and less effective. With primary school children, however, it is possible and necessary to ease this transition. Well designed structural material for the teaching of arithmetic and mathematics, for example, because it varies the way in which problems are presented, provokes different strategies for solving them. If the teacher knows what he is about, he can use this material to encourage the child to conceptualize, to ease the transition to symbolic manipulations, and to induce the development of increasingly generalized types of attack.

It has been shown, in a number of experiments, that children—even quite young children—are greatly helped if they verbalize as they look at the concrete presentation of their problem. This seems to be because verbalization helps to designate, to discriminate and to classify. Children remember objects better if they name them than if they simply put a ring round the word designating them; they will learn better if they accompany their learning as they go with verbal formulations of what they acquire; they will solve problems better if they talk aloud while they are doing them. This suggests that it is likely to be helpful (in many cases, though not perhaps in all) to stimulate discussion of the problem by the children before they attempt to solve it. With older children it is worth while asking them to formulate on paper an analysis of the problem and to set up a plan of attack. It can also be helpful to the teacher since, if the child fails to formulate the problem clearly and correctly, diagnosis of his difficulty is much easier. Katona and others have shown that diagrammatic or graphical representation will also help in the solution of certain types of problems. Williams gives a good example, here, which is quoted because it illustrates how certain types of diagrammatic presentation will help. The problem is of the familiar type: 'John gave Joe twice as much as Jim gave George' (the alliteration is there, of course, as a distractor); 'Joe gave George half of what he received; if Jim gave George sixpence, how much did George receive altogether?' If this is dealt with diagrammatically, many people will find it easily solvable who might otherwise have found it difficult.

This calls, of course, for a simple type of diagrammatic representation and is not a unique way of attack; but there are other problems which can be solved only in this way. The research work on problem solving suggests that there are individual differences in the usefulness of diagrammatic techniques and, of course, differences inherent in the types of problem. In any case, however, it nearly always helps, with a complicated problem, to list the items of information in some patterned way and try these patterns out. No method is likely to work with all problems, with all children and every time.

Finally, a good deal of work suggests that group methods of problem solving may also be useful. The advantage of this form of attack is that many more hypotheses tend to be thrown up by a group than one person would be likely to think of: groups are more productive of hypotheses and therefore are likely to be more productive of solutions than single persons, though in fact they take more time. The solutions reached tend to have a higher quality; a matter of importance when you are confronted by problems which have no right, absolute and unique solution. There tends also to be a higher level of criticism of the hypotheses and of the solutions in a group. This technique has obvious educational value, especially in teaching children how to solve more complex types of problem, particularly those which do not have the inherent simplicity of mathematics but are more 'real' in the sense that they touch the untidiness of life. Attention should, however, be drawn to another important and educationally valuable aspect. Within a group situation, it is possible to encourage the separation of the hypothesis forming from the evaluating type of activity. What one so often finds with children is that they have become so critical of their own powers that they are inhibited from producing a large number of hypotheses—good and bad—from which to choose. This may (and often does) mean they are inhibited from producing the apparently bizarre hypothesis which ultimately may be the right one. If a group is stimulated to throw everything into the ring as it were and to exercise critical choice only at a second stage, while much rubbish will be produced, much that is creative is enabled to reach the surface. The tasks of creation and criticism can be separated and trained separately with advantage.

This draws attention to a principal impediment to problem solving—anxiety. Anxiety seems to impair performance more in complex than in simple tasks. The fear of failure inhibits search and may prevent it altogether; over-confidence on the other hand tends to too facile types of acceptance. The problem, educationally, is that of how a child's morale can be maintained so that he will go through the stage of producing all sorts of hypotheses if these are required without feeling too critical about them and at a second stage he can be brought to exercise discrimination and judgement. If children are expected not to produce hypotheses which seem to be silly and if we criticize those which seem to be wild, we may in fact inhibit the more creative type of thought. This is one of the difficulties in the teaching of arithmetic. It does not permit of the bizarre type of hypothesis. The difficulty in teaching something like English is

74

that it does, but that it is difficult for children to have any means of judgement that is adequate. Between these two extremes lies the whole sequence of problems in the teaching of thinking.

We also know that if the problem is too difficult, the ensuing frustration will tend to constrictiveness and to reduction in fluency. The child will just cease to try. This means, obviously, that one tries to avoid the over-difficult type of problem; even more important is that one should make sure that the child confronted with a problem does have some sort of procedures which will enable him to get to grips with it. The understanding of techniques or procedures can be of two kinds: he may have a sufficient mastery of an appropriate technique in the sense that he can apply it; or he may understand the principles which underlie it. In the first case, provided the problem and technique fit, all will be well; but if there is an essential variation in the nature of the problem, then some understanding of underlying principles will be necessary to adapt the technique and make it serviceable.

This suggests that—even if it takes longer—children should be taught the rationale of the techniques they use and should experience wide differences in their application. Again, however, we must be neither simple minded nor absolute. Research seems to confirm common sense when it points out that, if you are dealing with intelligent children then it certainly pays to teach them the principles; but that if you are teaching duller children and over a fairly short term, it probably does not. A third proviso also turns up. If the generalization of the principles underlying a technique is too limited, this in itself may inhibit the intelligent child quite strongly. Finally, for our somewhat dubious comfort, it should be said that many intelligent children survive the wrong kind of teaching and develop wide and flexible strategies for themselves. This might lead us seriously to ask the question—relevant especially for opponents of any form of streaming, even of groups or sets within classes—whether it might be wise, in a class of widely varied ability, to teach all children problem-solving technique routines, in the hope that the dull ones would have something to get on with and the bright ones might be able to survive and surmount the routine. This, I suspect, would be a counsel of despair but it certainly looks as though some serious thought should be given to it by advocates of ultimate comprehensiveness.

Within any subject area we tend to teach the techniques of thinking, reasoning, problem solving, specifically appropriate to that area and we ignore or do not realize how far the techniques of one discipline, with slight or major alterations, are applicable elsewhere. Here again, it looks like educational sense to provide a wide variety of problems from different areas in the hope that, through the variety of techniques they are forced to apply, children will learn the common principles which underlie them. However, we must enter a caveat. If you have plenty of time, then it is probably better in the long run to proceed with plenty of variety. If time is short—if the examination is a fortnight away—then it is probably better and more economical to proceed with quite specific, more or less authoritarian, techniques for solving problems. The root of this is simple and commonplace enough; in using any particular technique a certain amount of practice is necessary; where you provide a variety of problems you of course tend to diminish the total amount of practice given on any one technique. The result, unless great care is exercised, is a width of partial mastery at the expense of real control though of many fewer techniques.

We are led to suggest to any teacher with any class that he makes clear to himself both the immediate and the ultimate aims he wishes to achieve in problem solving and that he carefully controls and records the length and type of practice which each child gets. This dazzling (but often ignored) glimpse of the obvious brings us to the question of whether children should discover or whether we should guide or even transmit discovery. There is a lot of educational cant about this. Some enthusiasts seem to say that children should be allowed to discover any old thing in any old way and we should hope for the best. This is tantamount to suggesting that in ten years, children will find out what it has taken, I suppose, several thousands of mankind to find out over centuries. At the other extreme are those who wish to instruct their pupils in everything which it is considered they should know and who believe that what sticks will be an intellectual capital for a life time. It is quite clear that genuine and effortless discovery leads children (and adults) to reorganize their information in newer and meaningful ways; that, in dealing with one problem situation successfully, they are likely to transfer what they more or less painfully acquire to similar new problems. But unguided discovery may lead even intelligent children to discovering inefficient techniques; and the partial success stamps these in. This again is like the tennis player who teaches himself and can never get beyond a certain level because the skills he has, as it were, over-practised inhibit the learning of higher level or more effective ones. Once more research confirms common sense. Discovery by itself is likely to be much less useful educationally than discovery plus guidance. Practically, this seems to mean that the teacher does not tell the child how to solve the problem but that he asks leading questions, he gives hints, he arranges the situation so that the child in fact tumbles into discovery by an effective route. Cross-evidence, however, suggests caution. It seems that a permissive atmosphere tends to favour the intelligent and a more prescriptive and directive one the less intelligent. This is in slight contradiction of some modern philosophies of education and I am not going to take sides, except to say that there are degrees of permissiveness. Practically, it is sometimes necessary, with not very bright children, to give them the security of a good deal of directiveness and then to proceed by questioning and hinting. How far this is done is a matter for the sensitivity of the teacher to the level at which the child is and how far he is motivated to tumble over into a solution.

So far little has been said about the way in which emotion may directly falsify reasoning and problem solving—a matter of the utmost importance educationally. It seems to me evident that we have to do something in education about the impact of prejudice and rigidity, and about emotionally determined blocks on reasoning. Here the general suggestion may be made that we should see to it that education confronts pupils not merely with variety within the type of problem but with a variety of kinds and areas of problems from the unique solution type we find in mathematics to the compromise solution type which in fact is characteristic of almost every kind of problem outside mathematics. There are in fact few human problems which have a uniquely determinable solution; and it is important that the real problems of the classroom—disciplinary problems, personal problems—and as you get on into adolescence, ethical and other kinds of problems—should be attacked in a problem solving and not in a didactic kind of way. Secondly—and this too is particularly true at adolescence—it is important to make the technique for solving all kinds of problem *explicit* and to show that these techniques can be transferred: that the kind of mental process which goes on in looking at a mathematical problem is in fact generically similar to the more complex processes and strategies demanded by personal and social problems. It is worth while, for example, to get children to write down the pro's and con's of some problem which vexes them. It is worth while trying to get them to set up, on this basis, a series of hypotheses, in imagination, in real situations. It is worth while indicating to them that there are differing degrees of rigour in the way in which people use language and that very often words which seem to be just words conveying items of information or facts, may be heavily emotionally charged. 'Race' may be taken as an obvious example to show how a word may have a meaning apart from its intellectual content and how, in any discussion, this emotional content will tend to interfere with objective thought.

While language is perhaps the most evident area in which this occurs, it can occur in other forms of symbolization. In this connection it is worth while giving practice in the transposition of statements and reasoning on problems charged with emotion from verbal to other symbolisms; and similarly that of turning visual material into words. I once came across an interesting piece of research, which I have never succeeded in finding again, in which propositions were put in two ways: in the first, statements were put in symbolic form —all A are B, therefore all B are A, with a request to mark them true or false. Then, in the second part of the test, statements of similar logical form were expressed in words with highly charged emotional contents—for example, 'all communists are trade unionists, therefore all trade unionists are communists'. It was found, even with quite intelligent university graduates, that the interference of the emotionally charged presentation was marked. They were American university students, of course, and I am sure that this would not happen here: we never see any examples of this in the press or anywhere else!

Finally, it is worth while to draw attention to the fact that any hypothesis, if it is to be something more than a pious opinion, must be put in a form that permits verification. Vague definitions, rolling phrases ('good citizens', 'high standards of moral behaviour') have to be made precise and put in operational terms before they can be verified. In this, in most of the areas of life that count, prejudice and emotion tend to colour and distort. Hence perhaps the most critical task of all for education is that of training pupils to reflect upon their own thought processes and particularly upon the way in which prejudices may colour their choice of problems; the kinds of data which they are prepared to admit as part of the solution; and how such factors influence the evaluation of the solution once they have arrived at it. This seems to me to be eminently a job for the teacher of adolescents, but it is not solely his. Young children suffer from emotional distortions—and so, of course, do their teachers.

4

HARRY KAY

Programmed learning

Over the last five years there has been an amazing transformation in the field of programmed instruction and teaching machines. In 1960 our Psychology Department at Sheffield was the first in this country to receive a government grant for research in programmed learning. The available literature was then so meagre and we received so many requests for information that we twice duplicated and distributed our own Bulletin to supply the need. By contrast, at the beginning of this month a booklet of ours entitled *Teaching Machines* was published by the Stationery Office and we could refer to a dozen or more full texts, four journals and innumerable articles such as those in *The Times Educational Supplement*, *B.A.C.I.E. Journal* and so on. I think those of us who have been in this work from the beginning in this country feel a little exhausted by the pace of what has happened. Those who have had anything useful to say have had to say it all too often, and those who may have had less to say have been no less frequent. Four years ago, if we discussed programmed instruction with publishers there was a detached, almost patronizing interest in its novelty, whereas now almost anything with the name 'programme' on it is published. Several, to my mind, are in print which never ought to be. The dictum is Thurber's, 'Don't get it right, just get it written.'

I think we would agree that for any idea to have made such an impression in so short a time, and in such an old established field as education, there must be coincidence of two features. Firstly, there must be a demand for it, and secondly, the idea itself must be able, at some level, to produce evidence that it will meet the need.

I have deliberately put the need as the first priority. Teaching machines have not a long history but in the past thirty years this present development marks their second appearance. When Pressey first tried to interest the world in them in the 1920's he found, and quite rightly so, that you cannot sell teaching machines to a community with teachers on the dole. I think, even more significantly, that you cannot sell machines and new ideas to a society that is looking backwards. Only in a world which is alive to challenge, and is demanding instruction in a whole range of new subjects, do you have a willingness to turn to new methods. Where there are so many established traditions, as in Britain, there is an understandable but handicapping reluctance to change.

What of the idea itself? Has it any obvious face validity or has it progressed by the sheer weight of supporting evidence? There are many interesting points here. Teachers have used machines of one kind or another for a long time. The system began when the first message was scratched in the sand. Man had learned to communicate without the actual presence of an audience. It is not surprising after so many centuries that the modern textbook is such a superbly designed machine. It would be hard to get more information into it. But its virtue is that it contains information and not necessarily that it communicates it. We all have books on our shelves which, alas, some day we are going to read. You can bring a student to a book but you cannot make him read. In a recent paper Professor Skinner quoted an interesting comment from Thorndike, written in 1912: 'If by a miracle of mechanical ingenuity a book could be so arranged that only to him who had done what was directed on page one could page two become visible, and so on, much that now requires personal instruction could be managed by print.'

The idea, then, was there in 1912 but the demand, the

urgency, was not, and it flickered away. Now it is alight again. During the 1940's simulators had been used for a variety of training tasks. Machines had been widely employed for presenting information and asking questions. A new concept of a machine had been born. The fixed and rigid image of a mechanized era had given way to the flexible and adaptive concept of an electronic decade. The fifties in America were able to take in their stride the idea that machines could teach —an example of America in its turn redressing the balance of the old world of human teachers by calling in a new world of machines.

I think it is important that we appreciate this liberation in outlook, whether we agree with it or not. I want to consider a little later why I think the subject has not developed exactly as might have been expected, but even so I think this attitude towards machines may *eventually* be the most important factor in the history of teaching methods. We have here in education yet another example of what is happening in other fields such as communications, transport, assembly and planning operations.

We would all accept that teaching machine methods are control systems in transmitting information. They are part and parcel of the general developments in communications which we have witnessed. The ordinary classroom procedure is primarily a one way transmission system with the good teacher doing his best to make it two way. In a public lecture such as this, it can only be one way. I may have 'lost' you (listener or reader) in the first minute—fortunately for my ego, I shall never know. In the tutorial with a limited student population the tutor tries to exercise more control. He asks questions. There is a give and take of information, and, in the best tutorials, neither party is allowed to hold the floor too long—the other might doze off.

As soon as we try to replace the human teacher with some defined agent we appreciate the flexibility of, and the many roles played by, the human teacher. We have to be content with a specified subject-matter store, we have to ensure that we can cater for the response of the student and that we can evaluate it. But immediately this limitation brings out a key feature of programmed instruction. Most systems for reasons of economy cannot build large subject-matter stores, and so, in consequence, the programmer has to specify exactly what it is he wishes to teach. There is no room here for sloppiness. The programmer must know what his students have already learned, what terms are familiar to them and what will be new. This must be precise. It is not enough for the programmer to ask, say, the teacher, how much of a subject the class is supposed to know. (The popular idea of programmers now is that if a teacher says a class knows a particular point, then 30 per cent may do so.) The programmer begins by finding out.

The whole of programming continues in this strictly empirical way. Having identified the present abilities of his students and knowing exactly what he is aiming to teach the programmer starts arranging his subject matter in what seems to him the best order of presentation. He examines the relationships of the items he intends to teach by a systematic analysis and this sometimes brings about a restructuring of a subject. He then tries writing the individual frames and again refers them to the students. He finds out whether the frames are saying to others what he believes them to say. And as soon as he has a sequence of intelligible frames he tries them on a sample of students. Gradually out of this constant evaluation of the material is created a set of frames that does teach satisfactorily.

General purpose teaching machines—the Auto Tutor, the Grundytutor, the Empirical Tutor, our own Sheffield machine—are entirely dependent upon the quality of their programmes. When different kinds of programme were first put forward such as Skinner's Linear or Crowder's Branching system it was popular to contrast them as if they represented totally different systems. Their differences are probably less important than was thought—what they have in common is far more relevant. I prefer to discuss all their qualities under two headings. First, as already noted, they are the result of a continuous evaluative procedure. What is finally presented is the result of an interaction between programmer and student, in which the final word is with the student. This programme is not satisfactory just because I, as the programmer, think it is, or because the student thinks it is, but because it has been verified that this programme does teach particular students what it was designed to teach. This evaluation should be the same for all kinds of programmes and semi-pejorative terms such as 'intrinsic' and 'extrinsic' should be dropped from the programming vocabulary. They are totally misleading.

Secondly, the whole procedure is a form of active learning. The programme is designed to function with the maximum participation by the student. Each frame seeks a response. It is so different from the lecture or classroom procedure where information rolls out and the body of students rolls to sleep. Here after only one step the student is manipulating what he has learned. He reads another step and further responses are required. It has been put together to teach him, not to baffle him and it is directed by his active participation. As the student goes to sleep so does the machine.

It may seem surprising how little was known, and is known, about programmes. Even today you hear bandied around such popular misconceptions as 'Programmes are best for teaching rote information. They should be used only for communicating facts.' This was not an implausible assumption, but results indicate that it is not true. Programmes have been more successful in teaching subjects where it was essential that students should *understand* the subject matter. This is not unexpected. The programme tries to build up a student's comprehension, to guide him and not baffle him. The title 'Teaching Machines' has so often created an image of a robot, and gives the impression of being a somewhat slick way of meeting the serious problem of teaching. Yet as every programmer has discovered, the exercise of constructing a programme could not be more painstaking. Again no one is trying to claim that the best of all possible methods is now known. Different procedures for the analysis of material are being tried, and from such studies it is hoped a permanent contribution may be made to the art of communicating.

But you have asked me to speak as a research worker in this field. 'What now follows?' It is tempting to be starry eyed, to envisage the computer in the classroom, handling the problems of each student separately, and providing guidance to each. When that time comes the hard grind of programme writing as we know it today will be cut and a lot more will be left to the machine. Such developments will be attempted if only for the reason mentioned earlier that we have begun to appreciate the adaptability of machines. Research experiments in the United States have already shown the possibilities here. Even so, I am certain that it will be a long time before anything of this kind will be current in this country. What then may the possible developments be in the immediate future?

I wish to discuss one possibility and I should stress that it is purely a personal opinion. I appreciate this view is not necessarily held by colleagues in this field, and I recognize that it may be a shock to some of them.

It seems to me that one development of teaching machines and programmes may be quite different from what has happened so far. Teaching machines have always stressed that they are designed to teach the individual student who will proceed at his own pace. The point to notice here is that teaching machines are deliberately running counter to the trend of so many modern communication systems to reach bigger numbers of students. Teaching machines stress the importance of the individual and there are good reasons why they should. To state only two, Skinner's work originated directly from the laboratory where everything had been reinforced on an individual basis. Branching systems for their part were analogous to the tutorial situation where again the tutor confronts an individual student.

But as research reports have accumulated a different emphasis has emerged. As we have seen, Pressey was able to discuss his early teaching machines with hardly any mention of what went inside them—the programmes. Today they are accepted as the core of the system. It has been realized that programmes are not something dreamed up by an inspired research worker or teacher. They are, as we have seen, a systematic presentation of material designed to teach a specific subject to a specific class of students. But above all they become a teaching instrument because they have been forged by an evaluation where frames that have not communicated successfully have been rejected and where a final programme accepts only those sequences which have been demonstrated to teach. The concept of testing the student has given way to that of testing the programme, and only when it has been demonstrated to be successful is it allowed to teach. Programmes have been found to achieve a far greater measure of control than their originators had expected, and even when used without the added control of a machine, they were still effective teaching instruments. It had not been foreseen how efficient a programme could be when so much care had been put into its design, and so much effort made to evaluate it with students.

From this there emerge consequences which were probably not expected by any of us at first. We had forged a new weapon for teaching students. But if this weapon were as good as we now discovered it to be, were we correct in trying to restrict its usage to individuals? This issue is probably the most controversial that could be raised in the field of programmed instruction and indeed so much has been written of the virtues of teaching machines giving individual instruction that it may seem presumptuous to bring up the question. But let us ask, 'Why individual instruction? Why have programmers emphasized that this is such an asset?' There seem to be several answers, some of substance and some less so. Individual instruction, particularly as practised in the older universities in the tutorial system, enjoys considerable prestige. This method has definitely been successful. Perhaps of more relevance are the kinds of objections that Skinner has made to class instruction, namely that a human teacher cannot possibly meet the individual requirements of many students at the same time. Hence in a large group, some students' responses are not confirmed nor is there any continuity between their error responses to the last item and the material that follows. This is a basic criticism. If the individual student has not followed the material he may easily be 'lost' and the remainder of the lesson is of no value to him. It is here that the philosophy of teaching machines is most challenging, for it has reversed the modern trend to adhere to open-loop systems whereby larger and larger numbers may be taught from a single source.

In adopting a closed-loop system teaching machines have deliberately run counter to this trend and have reiterated a cardinal point of teaching, namely, that the accent should be more on what a student receives than what is transmitted. They have performed a magnificent service in emphasizing that teaching is an exercise in the controlled transmission of information, whilst their method of making a student respond at each step and then taking appropriate action on the response is one of the surest methods of achieving this. But the assumption that this control can *only* be achieved by presenting one display to one student and receiving one response from him may not follow, and may indeed be only a relic from a preprogramming tradition. For example, if we are using a linear programme where the same sequence of material is presented to all students, why should we not offer all of them individual facilities for responding and present the material to them as a group? I think reluctance to do this has arisen partly from a lack of confidence of what can be achieved by programme evaluation. Where material has first been carefully arranged in sequence and then subsequently amended after being tried out upon a sample of students, a much more efficient teaching instrument has been designed than the ordinary classroom lesson. If it is still the aim that a high proportion of responses should be correct, then a firm measure of control may still be exercised over teaching in this group situation. I feel that this is now a question for research. If it is possible to achieve efficient results in such a group situation, its implications are widespread, particularly in those developing countries which could hardly afford the luxury of individual instruction.

It is also worth pointing out that the consequences of a group situation need not all be negative. There are some advantages to be gained. For example, if a group is homogeneous, motivation may be increased by giving some indication of group results. A possible system is to score individual responses so that each student knows the results of his own response but also knows how well the group as a whole has performed. This can be conveniently given in the form of a percentage score for the group, immediately all the members have responded. In this way the group is interested both in the speed and accuracy of its members' responses. Such suggestions might be examined empirically.

It may be objected that a group situation would not permit each student to proceed at his own pace. There are certain advantages in a student setting his own pace, but again it may have drawbacks. We are considering programmed instruction as a control system in the transmission of information. The novelty is not in the machine *per se*, but in a system which tries to control teaching at each step. The practice of presenting material in small units to which a student has to respond is the basis of a simple closed-loop system which has much to recommend it. But most closed-loop systems in communicating engineering have some time constraints imposed upon them. For example, if feed-back information were subject to delay this would often render it valueless. There is a time relationship between response and feed back which must be preserved.

Yet it is a feature of much teaching machine practice that there are no time constraints. Each individual student may inspect material for as long as he wishes and take as long as he likes over his response. Since it is well known that some individuals can make their responses much faster than others the system has an obvious virtue in catering for these differences and, as we all know, rate of learning is a key feature of Skinner's work. But the lack of control which varying time intervals introduce may be more of a disadvantage than has been realized. For example, in preparing a programme certain average speeds of progress have to be envisaged. It makes a considerable difference if the student is to go through the material in two days or two weeks, apart from influencing the number of revision frames which are necessary. In one of our studies middle-aged students were in fact spending over two hours on a short lesson designed for forty minutes. In cases such as this the continuity between frames may be lost if the time interval which elapses between them is too great.

It is my experience as a research worker conducting experiments on learning that subjects do not always choose the most advantageous time for themselves. Often their performance may be improved by externally pacing their work. If, as teachers, or programmers, we assume the responsibility of designing how material shall be presented, ought we not to accept the further responsibility of presenting it for a certain length of time?

There are a few teaching machines which do exercise some form of pacing. S.A.K.I. (Self-Organizing Automatic Keyboard Instructor) for example, operates on two main variables, the accuracy of a response and its latency. It is interesting that a time measure of the delay taken in giving the correct response should be a useful index of how well a task has been learned.

Another example is a simple form of programmed reading machine. The word to be read is printed on the back of a magnetic tape which moves very slowly on a tape recorder. The printed word is visible for a prescribed and a predictable period to a student. It then passes from his view. In certain conditions the tape recorder will 'play' the word whilst it is being visually presented, in other conditions the auditory presentation is given after the visual presentation and when the student has had time to respond. With this procedure a student knows there is a limited time in which to perceive the signal and to make a response. It will be valuable to know what success is achieved with a machine which specifies when and for how long a subject should attend to a particular frame.

My argument then is that if programmed instruction provides the controlled teaching of the kind we have discussed it could be used with groups of students. I think that once we begin to ask the question about group instruction we appreciate that there are many reasons why programmes should succeed with a class where a less prepared lesson, demanding less participation from the student, would fail. You will appreciate that what I am advocating here is no fantasy, costing astronomical sums. Let me be as practical as possible and suggest how it might operate.

If we think of an ordinary classroom each pupil could be provided with a small keyboard say of four keys and an indicator light. The keys are connected to a central control panel. If required a student may work in a booth as in some language laboratories. The programme would be projected by standard 35 mm. film using single frame exposure. Each frame calls for a response which the student makes by pressing one of the keys. This immediately illuminates one of the lights in the central control panel and also gives an indicator light to tell the student whether he is correct or not. It is a simple matter to score each student's response so that the score of the whole class can also be presented. When all the class members have responded the programme is stepped on to the next frame.

It would not be an elaborate exercise to make such a device. It would, for example, require much less equipment than the language laboratory. One projector unit per class would be enough. I don't know of any such equipment in Britain but there is, in the Chesterfield Technical College, an admirable mechanized classroom in which 2 in. × 2 in. slide projection is controlled by the teacher, and the students' responses are recorded from a central console. It seemed to me to provide an admirable indication to the teacher of how the students were progressing.

In my own Department we intend to continue research on programmes with group instruction with mechanized classrooms. No research worker can guarantee results—it would not be research if he could—but I believe there is a definite contribution to be made in this field. An investigation into programmed instruction on a group basis would be one of the most sensible projects that any Ministry in this country could support. Again, for manufacturers who are interested, the possibilities are particularly attractive for programmed instruction to a class is surely the answer for developing countries.

I have tried in this lecture to consider in the light of its theoretical approach, and with the added wisdom of hindsight, how we might modify assumptions that have hitherto directed our thinking about programming. Yet the immediate benefit we have gained from teaching machines and programmes is that they have made so many think again about the job of teaching. They have put the accent where it should be—on teaching. One of the crucial arguments now is how far can we progress in teaching average students. There are a lot of them! It is only too easy for newspaper leaders to sniff at the Robbins report, anticipating a fall in standards with increasing numbers of students. And yet in so many spheres of activity where we can measure accurately the evidence is clear enough. Where there is a yardstick records are apparently made to be broken; but where there is no yardstick, nothing is as good as it was. Human endeavour in so many fields is attaining more—why not in the field of education?

5

BEN MORRIS

How Does a Group Learn to Work Together?

Introduction

It is doubtful whether the question I have been asked to discuss is as yet capable of being given a very precise answer. As posed it is a very broad question with diverse implications and it could entice us into an alarmingly complex field, a field embracing large parts of sociology and social psychology. I therefore intend drastically to simplify the issues, and in the first place I propose to limit myself to a consideration of small face-to-face groups and to consider only some aspects of these. In doing so, it would seem obvious that the most relevant aspects to select for emphasis are those which can be easily related to learning and teaching, as these terms are understood in our schools and colleges. And what might seem certain obvious distinctions, I intend to disregard. For example the difference between children and adults learning to work together is one I shall make light of, since however various the implications for practice, the same basic principles apply in both cases. Again, a group may exist either to enhance the learning of individuals or primarily for the sake of collective action and a collective product or for both purposes as in project work. When the emphasis is on individual learning in a group situation, the formation of a group, effective as a group, is usually a necessary, although it may not be a sufficient, condition for optimum individual learning. I shall therefore emphasize the factors concerned with the effective functioning of a group as such.

What importance is to be attached to the task a group is trying to accomplish? What difference does it make whether the task is simply discussion, or solving a mathematical problem or making a boat? So far as essential principles are concerned I think the particular nature of the task makes little difference and again I shall ignore such questions.

Even these limitations however are not sufficient. A small group is always part of a larger social structure, its institutional or societal setting. The class is part of the school, and larger and smaller units always influence and are influenced by each other. For the most part I intend deliberately to ignore the larger aspects of social structure, i.e. those normally dealt with by sociologists, including here even those that may quite directly influence small group membership and behaviour, such as social class. Further, a group is composed of individuals and the way in which a group learns is greatly influenced by the personalities of its members and by the way in which each of them learns as an individual. But the psychology of learning as ordinarily dealt with by psychologists, when thinking in terms of the individual, I shall also have to exclude. By largely ignoring sociology and individual psychology, no disrespect to these disciplines is intended. The omission is merely a device to render our topic manageable. Because of these restrictions however the treatment I can give our theme is bound to be far from thorough.

What then is the focus of my discussion? It is a consideration of small groups, their purposes, both objectively given and subjectively perceived by their members, and the interpersonal relations of the members among themselves. Nevertheless it is not in fact possible to come to grips even with the essentials of group learning in this restricted sense without going further afield in one particular direction and discussing some fundamental issues in human relations. Before doing so however it might be instructive to glance at the history of our topic.

The deliberate use of small groups in education, industry, psychotherapy and other fields is one of the most marked tendencies in social practice in this country since World War II. One interesting question to raise would be as to why this has been so; another would be to inquire how we may discriminate between soundly based procedures on the one hand and developments which savour of the operations of a 'cult' on the other. The word 'group' has indeed, as sometimes used, come to surround itself with an aura of 'mystique' and it might be important, although perhaps only incidentally, to do something to dispel such accretions.

It seems quite often to be assumed, erroneously, that group techniques in education and social affairs originated in our war-time world. Certainly the war and its aftermath gave a great impetus to their use, and in England this was largely as a result of the work of the Army Bureau of Current Affairs and of the War Office Selection Boards. It is important in this connection however to recall the pioneer studies of J. L. Moreno and Kurt Lewin and his associates in the U.S.A. in the middle and late thirties respectively since these soon began to have an influence on this side of the Atlantic. This work itself was also influenced by the social and intellectual climate between and even before the wars, as represented by such influential figures as Floyd Allport, Mary Parker Follett and Elton Mayo for example and by their forerunners, McDougall, Trotter and Le Bon. Moreover certain experiments in industrial organization and management had a significant fertilizing effect, notably those carried out at the Western Electric Company's works at Hawthorne, Chicago, in which the startling truth was discovered that to take an interest in people as human beings, rather than as production units, has a far greater effect on morale and productivity than any combination of incentives, rest pauses, or time and motion saving devices!

A moment's further reflection shows that group techniques have a long history. Socrates used a version of group discussion for educational purposes, and group procedures were used to conduct village affairs for example in Russia and in India from ancient times. In the Western world, the Society of Friends developed them in one particular direction to a high pitch of efficiency. Such examples, and they are only examples of widespread practices, might well repay careful scrutiny in any more detailed study. In their modern form I first met group procedures for learning in the Education Department of Glasgow University, where between the wars the late Dr. William Boyd, again I think under American influence, employed small group tutorial methods with a staff-student ratio of about 1 to 50. This was accomplished by setting groups of about 10 students to discuss specific questions and the staff sharing out their time among the groups. Have we as yet, I wonder, fully exploited this particular method in our higher educational institutions in this country? Should we not pay special attention to it in the post Robbins era, remembering that it is estimated that the percentage of the age group entering full-time higher education will double in the next twenty years (Robbins 1963)?

The Study of Small Groups

There are various ways of formulating the main features of a working group. Homans (1951) as summarized by Sprott (1958) says this:

'People do not just get together; they get together for a purpose. There are motives for each member to join a group, there are the activities which the group engages in, and there are the interactions between the members which the activities of the group bring about. These three factors, sentiment (which includes original motives and those derived during the group activities), activity and interaction are interrelated. If you alter any of them, you will alter the other two.'

I would put the matter a little differently and say this. In a group which has learned to work together effectively, we may pre-suppose both a common purpose and a high degree of member participation. But the appeal of a common purpose and the degree of member participation depend primarily on the inter-personal relations ('interactions' in behaviourist language) of group members. What then are the factors which mediate inter-personal relations in a group?

Pioneer studies and controlled experimental work into experience and behaviour in small groups may broadly speaking be divided into three major lines of development; firstly, Sociometric (including psycho-dramatic and socio-dramatic) studies stemming from the work of Moreno (1934), secondly, studies in Group Dynamics by various workers in the U.S.A. and developed by Lewin (1947–48), his associates and their pupils; and thirdly, psycho-analytically oriented group work initiated by Bion, Rickman, Bridger, Foulkes and others in the British Army (Bion 1946). This work was subsequently developed by Bion and his associates at the Tavistock Clinic and Tavistock Institute of Human Relations (Tavistock 1946–47), and independently by other psycho-analysts, notably Foulkes and Anthony (1957). All three lines of development have made important contributions to our present theme, and perhaps not surprisingly, considering the nature of these studies, all three have been and are beset by dangers of over-elaboration and of uncontrolled enthusiasm. As always, of course, such dangers and difficulties may contribute much to our understanding.

In this field it is not possible to reach general conclusions by referring only to selected specific studies. We must rely on the cumulative evidence of many studies. It is important therefore at this point to consider briefly each of the three main areas of work I have indicated, since between them they call attention to some of the fundamental factors involved in co-operative behaviour in groups, and each introduces us to a large body of evidence.

I SOCIOMETRIC STUDIES

In any group of adults or children in practical association

with one another, there exist complicated patterns of attraction, repulsion and neutrality. These patterns have potentially at their command the large reservoirs of feeling to be found in every individual. It was J. L. Moreno (loc. cit.) who first made these facts effectively clear and it was he who systematically developed the simple procedure known as the 'sociometric test'—in which group members express their preferences for each other in terms of companionship or working partnership—to provide maps or charts of the interrelations between group members. By means of such a device the truly popular members of a group (those around whom preferences cluster), the less popular ones, and the isolates (those rejected by the majority) can readily be spotted, and such information can provide a teacher with a factual basis on which to build a policy for grouping pupils within a class. An actual policy for grouping however, requires more than sociometric facts; clear aims, experience, insight and the results of other kinds of researches are also required.

The work of Moreno greatly influenced Dr. C. M. Fleming and her students in this Institute in their studies of the use of group techniques, particularly in the education of the adolescent. For example, Richardson (1951) showed that an experimental group learning English by group methods showed significant gains in co-operative attitudes and in attainments, over a comparable control group conventionally taught. This work draws attention to the important but apparently (in educational circles) forgotten fact that the most effective and most satisfying group in which to work is a group of friends. In more general terms, the existence of positive emotional ties between group members is a *sine qua non*, not only of a feeling of unity but of each member playing a full part in co-operative activity. When such ties already exist, teaching should make wise use of them. When they do not, the use of group methods, guided by a judicious use of sociometric data, may help considerably to bring them into being. Learning to work together in a group is therefore both dependent on the existence of co-operative relations and may

G

be conducive to their further development. The limitations of sociometric studies for our immediate purpose are two fold (they have of course other purposes). They do not in themselves lead to any great deepening of understanding of the factors underlying the growth or decline of co-operative attitudes, and when pursued to the bitter end rapidly lead into a maze of complexities without corresponding gains in practical application.

2   GROUP DYNAMICS

It would obviously be valuable if we could understand in greater detail how behaviour in a group is affected by the personal characteristics of its members, by different kinds of leadership, by different kinds of structure and institutional setting and by different tasks and purposes. Studies which aim at such understanding may conveniently be labelled under the term 'group dynamics'. In the hands of Kurt Lewin and his senior associates such studies have thrown into sharp relief the functions and modes of leadership and the basic behaviour patterns to be observed in the interactions of group members. The, by now, classical studies of group climates by Lippett and White (1943) have proved immensely stimulating of further research and have also, I may say, proved a great boon to lecturers in social psychology! Rigid contrasts between authoritarian, so-called democratic participation, and 'laissez-faire' exercise of leadership, certainly over-simplify complex situations, but the superiority of a climate of democratically guided participation over other climates, as regards solidarity, learning, and productivity, is now generally accepted.

One danger into which such work has run is that of over-elaborate situational analysis in purely behaviouristic terms in severely simplified laboratory conditions. This is liable to result in a form of intellectual sterility. Another danger, in the hands of insufficiently trained and over-enthusiastic practitioners, is that of degeneration into a 'cult' of group dynamics, which appears to have been rather widespread in the U.S.A. at one time. Moreover by seeking to control the conditions and influences under which people work, an almost inevitable component of stage management enters the proceedings. Thus an even more serious danger which haunts this type of work is that of the deliberate manipulation or control of the feelings and behaviour of others. Charges of this kind levelled against 'group dynamicists' are by no means all baseless. But just as in all other aspects of applied social science, the answer to the question whether actions are to be regarded as manipulative or not depends essentially on both the motives and the intentions of those carrying them out. Of course, here as in all conduct, purity of heart is as difficult to define as to achieve.

3 PSYCHO-ANALYTICALLY ORIENTED STUDIES

It is from the psycho-analytically oriented work of W. R. Bion and his associates, however, that I personally think our most fundamental insights into group behaviour and learning have been gained. I may be prejudiced here since I am one of Bion's pupils, but his work seems to me to have a fundamental quality and an originality not found elsewhere, even in other psycho-analytically oriented group work. As his ideas developed Bion originated the type of group situation in which the group guided by a psycho-analytically experienced consultant is set the task, not of discussing a topic, or accomplishing an overt task, but of studying its own processes of member interaction. In this way a group gradually learns to recognize and to deal with the latent bonds of affection and hostility which exist within it. These 'study groups' as they have come to be called, originally had a purely psycho-therapeutic aim, but Bion himself perceived that they might have a valuable part to play in the training of educational, industrial and social welfare personnel. Several important practical developments have emerged from these beginnings, notably the industrial work of Jaques

(1951), Menzies (1960), Rice (1963) and others, the training courses in group relations organized jointly by the Tavistock Institute of Human Relations and Leicester University (Trist and Sofer 1959) and the pioneer studies in teacher training carried out by Herbert in Manchester (1961) and Richardson in Bristol (1963), to mention only a few about which reports have been published.

Since this type of work is concerned with fundamental motivation in human relationships it is liable to encounter dangers arising from the reactivation of powerful patterns of feeling first developed in infancy and childhood. One major danger, particularly in the hands of insufficiently trained group consultants (and also under unsuitable institutional arrangements) is that of allowing the tide of feeling in a group to rise to unmanageable proportions. What is liable to happen in these cases is that the group itself and/or its consultant becomes a 'loved object' on whom members become emotionally dependent, in much the same way and for similar reasons as a patient may become dependent on his analyst in certain phases of psycho-therapy. The loved object, that is, the group, then becomes 'over-valued' in the same sense as Freud used this term to describe the infantile attachment of a child to its parents, and also the state of affairs between ordinary people, when they are, as we say, in love with one another. This is one of the sources of 'group mystique', and groups in the grip of such mystique may for a time exhibit some of the characteristics of a secret sect or esoteric cult. Whether a psycho-analytically oriented group does or does not in fact exhibit such behaviour, charges of this kind are commonly levelled against it, for it is usually the object of considerable envy, just as people known or supposed to be lovers often are. A consultant who knows his job, however, can do much to help his group to work through such phases in its development, by appropriate and well-timed interpretations of behaviour within the group. Consultant and members alike however are also exposed to the constant danger of injudicious and over-elaborate interpretation.

This is a danger which it is extremely difficult to avoid and may be regarded, in the same way as over-valuation of the group or its consultant, as a necessary feature of development. Nevertheless one mark of the mature group consultant, as of the mature artist, is the economy of the means he uses. Like, for example, some of the great masters of jazz interpretation he will play remarkably few 'notes'. Clearly this is not a field of operation for amateurs.

The essence of this type of group work lies in the attempt to increase the insight of members into the unconscious dimension of inter-personal relations, with the purpose of enabling them to perceive more clearly what hinders and what helps the group to achieve greater effectiveness, and to act on their perceptions. Since responsibility for action is placed firmly on the group members themselves, this type of work, like psycho-analytic therapy itself, is in principle (if not always in practice) free from charges of manipulation. Different practitioners of such methods have, of course, different viewpoints, depending clearly on different aims. Foulkes, for example (loc. cit.), seems to exclude the use of transference interpretations, that is the explicit consideration of the unconscious relations between group members and the consultant, or conductor as he prefers to call him, while those who follow Bion make more or less use of such interpretations according to circumstances.

The practical claims made for this type of work are not easily submitted to examination by present-day conventional experimental methods, since these methods, as in the case of similar attempts to evaluate psycho-analytic therapy, usually entail destroying what one sets out to observe. As in psychotherapy, personal experience of such methods is an essential preliminary to their evaluation in any profound sense. The accounts of sessions published by Herbert and Richardson (loc. cit.) may however provide the curious outsider with some glimpses of what actually happens in such groups, even if such accounts fail to convince him of the validity, either of particular interpretations, or of the theoretical framework of interpretation itself. There exists no strong reason however for supposing either that all the benefits claimed by participants are always illusory, or that it should be a simple matter to identify and test the behavioural correlates of increased awareness. The actual practice of group work of this kind is in my view bound to be rather limited for technical reasons, one of them being the relatively short supply of properly trained group consultants and another being the nature of the functions it can perform. These seem to me primarily to be concerned with providing experiences through which people become more readily able to learn from more orthodox group situations. Its influence however may be far from limited. There are many who, like myself, although trained in such methods, prefer to use the insights gained in this training in the conduct of what appear to participants to be rather more conventional types of group discussion. But we must admit that the exact relationships between the various techniques and the conditions for their optimum use have not yet been fully worked out. From our present standpoint, the main significance of this work is theoretical and lies in the detailed suggestions it is able to make concerning the nature and function of the most fundamental factors in group co-operation.

To sum up this aspect of our discussion, we may say that all these three lines of work, the sociometric, the group dynamic and the psycho-analytically oriented, have in common a single central contribution to our theme of how a group learns to work together. They all emphasize the importance of emotional components in influencing member interaction within the group. They differ in their appeal to and emphasis upon group structure and leadership and in the extent to which they concern themselves with the latent and unconscious dimension of inter-personal relationships. A general conclusion to the effect that the operation of co-operative and unco-operative attitudes is at the heart of our problem is scarcely new. Rather it has become a hoary platitude. Yet this initial insight and its periodic rediscovery have been important aspects of the growth of human consciousness and many of the great philosophers of the past have discussed their implications. Kant, for example, held the view that man is by nature a being who can neither tolerate his fellow men nor get on without them. What modern experimental group studies contribute is detailed insight into the way in which various influences operate to control the balance between these attitudes. It is my own view that these various influences and the way in which they operate to unite and dis-unite the members of a working group may best be understood in terms of modern psycho-analytic theories of personality and inter-personal relations, and I therefore propose to consider a few of the concepts of this type of theory which seem to render the facts of group behaviour more intelligible than they otherwise would be.

Understanding Group Behaviour

In a sense the problem of how a group learns to work together is a bogus problem. The existence of a group presupposes co-operation, and there is no special problem of how, in principle, such co-operation is possible, apart from the general problem of the nature of human beings as such. It is probably true that only in a culture putting a high value on individuality could psychology develop as a theory of individual behaviour, and could co-operation present itself as a distinct theoretical problem. Yet a perfectly genuine scientific task does exist, namely the specification and explanation of the varieties of human interaction and the study of the influences which modulate it. How a group learns to work together well, rather than badly, is a genuine and very important problem. Dynamic theories of human behaviour nowadays begin from the facts of interdependence, of interaction, and seek to describe and explain human development and personality in terms of a theory of interpersonal relations (Guntrip 1961). We must therefore cast the problem of a group learning to work together in this form and see it in terms of the influences which modulate interpersonal relations.

I   INFLUENCES MODULATING INTERPERSONAL
RELATIONSHIPS

Essentially we are beings who develop by means of our relationships with one another, and are therefore in part constituted through these relationships. From their beginnings in the family, relationships are structured and coloured by feelings belonging to the great domains of love and fear, and the immediate derivative of fear, hate. In our dealings with one another in adult life, we are guided in the first instance by past experience, and therefore encounters between human beings are inevitably to some extent cast in a mould fashioned in the past, and of which we are in the present at best only dimly aware. The pattern of affection and unity on the one hand and of anxiety, rivalry, hostility and separateness on the other which we experienced in childhood tend to exercise considerable influence on the conduct of our adult affairs. At any stage we can best take advantage of opportunities for learning when these make use of patterns of relationships which recapitulate the patterns established as favourable to learning in the past.

At the same time throughout our development there is an element of anticipation—a search for an image of what we wish to and may become, i.e. a search for a personal identity. To be favourable, learning experiences should therefore connect easily with our aspirations and should provide us with roles which enable us to develop the kinds of relationships in terms of which our ideal self image is cast.

Influenced by the past, and anticipating the future, how do we become possessed of a sense of direction and a set of values for controlling our own behaviour? In laying the foundations of an ideal self and of a means of inner control, the primary raw materials are the personalities of our parents, the examples they provide, or rather our childish and therefore exaggerated versions of them as rewarding, frustrating and punishing figures. We make use of them by 'incorporating' or 'internalizing' them, and thus identifying ourselves with them. In so doing we come implicitly to accept their values. Thus in the very process of beginning to establish our own identity we acquire an internal sanctioning system, an internal authority or conscience which is a 'representative' of the external authority and values of the social group to which we belong. These images or representations of the external society in which we live are augmented through our relationships with other adults, with older companions and with contemporaries and they thus come to form an inner world or internal dimension of our being, which is largely unconscious and which is in constant interaction with the external world. While these influences exert a powerful influence upon us, they do not control our behaviour in its entirety, for in part our development consists in establishing the self as master in its own house, sensitive both to internal demands and promptings and to external pressures, and able to mediate between them. Nevertheless in all relationships unconscious and irrational components have a large part to play and these are very evident in group behaviour.

The shape our personalities take is therefore to a considerable extent a function of the relations we make with the people we meet—of what we call out in them and what they call out in us, be it love, fear or hate—or more usually, their subtle derivatives. Among ourselves we vary in our dependence on internal as against external authority, and each of us may vary in this way at different times and in different circumstances. In general however we tend to be either 'inner' or 'other' directed personalities (Riesman 1953). Seldom, however, are we collectively able to rely on inner direction alone; hence the need for rules, and for custom and for law. In most group situations we rely quite heavily, although often only implicitly (unconsciously), on various forms of external authority. When external authority is removed, even experimentally, our most immediate response is likely to be anxiety, since responsibility is then felt to be ours alone, and we are unsure how far we can trust ourselves and therefore others.

In attempting to understand the influences which modulate interpersonal relations and hence enter fundamentally into group experience, we have therefore to take into account an unconscious dimension of ourselves, an inner world, having its roots in the past and oriented toward the future, in terms of which we attempt to interpret and deal with present reality. Where this reality consists of other people in a group situation, each with an inner world of his or her own, we can see that the achievement of a common purpose depends on the acceptance by each member of an inner representation of authority which is common to and acknowledged by all.

2   PARTICIPATION AND THE COMMON TASK

Within groups, either spontaneously formed for a specific purpose, or brought together and given a common task by a teacher or leader, the role of the common task would seem to be the obvious one of forming a focus of endeavour. It can do this however only in so far as it offers a goal which is sufficiently clear and close to the interests of members, i.e. offers them roles sufficiently in conformity with their past experience and with aspects of their self image. Its capacity to do this is in turn also partly dependent on whether it can allow them to 'sink their differences' and abandon their purely private objectives. Therefore a task which appeals sufficiently to all—to 'where the members are' that is, to their past experience, their current interests and abilities and to their aspirations—is essential. Neglect of these conditions is the cause of many educational failures, failure for example to engage the enthusiasm of adolescent groups. Equally, successful experiments in youth work all exemplify this condition. In bringing into being an acceptable common task and in maintaining interest in it, both the skill and the personality of the leader are of great significance. Often at first, both with young children and with adolescents, it is the leader himself who is the real focus rather than the task. For the group to grow however, intrinsic interests which are separable from the personality of the leader must emerge. If this does not happen, the group becomes wholly dependent on the leader, and its future is thereby endangered; for groups, like individuals, if they are to survive, have eventually to be weaned.

Where a group has to find or be given a task, this task can seldom be adequately formulated beforehand, or even immediately the group is convened. A leader who attempts totally to define and to circumscribe the common task himself, is failing to offer adequate opportunities for participation to the members. By ignoring the important contributions that they may be able to make, he is lessening the chance of discovering a task sufficiently in conformity with their interests to call out their full enthusiasm. And by so doing he is likely to strengthen hostilities within the group and toward himself through the growth of a sense of frustration among the members. Such frustrations would seem to underlie the comparative failure of some meetings and conferences. When the agenda is laid down with complete rigidity and everything is decided beforehand and 'from above', the private 'agendas', i.e. purposes, abilities, problems and aspirations of participants are being ignored instead of constructively used. The same may be said of educational programmes which seriously curtail or eliminate the potential contributions of the learners. We may notice however that this criterion of participation does not necessarily condemn the formal lecture as is sometimes mistakenly concluded. The question to be asked about the lecture is the place it should occupy in a structured system of varied learning situations.

The role of a definite common task and/or definite leadership is nowhere made clearer than when a group is asked to define its own task or proceed without a leader. Leaderless groups can of course learn to work together, but usually only by finding a leader or leaders from among themselves, or, unless they all happen already to be friends, by going through a fairly long period of exploration and decision making. In appropriate circumstances such an experience can be very valuable in learning more about how groups function and what makes for effective communication and common action. Whether circumstances are favourable for this depends primarily on the aim of the whole exercise and on the time available for it. The removal of external authority, either in the form of an overt task and/or the presence of a recognized leader who is prepared to act as such, is nearly always accompanied by the appearance of anxiety within the group, anxiety very often expressed in hostile behaviour. Except in special circumstances and with experienced groups, the 'internal authority' residing within each member is not trusted to produce order and prevent chaos. Members fear the irruption of their own private imperious purposes, and those of others. Thus neither excessive authority from a leader nor its entire absence are conducive to effective co-operation in most circumstances.

It is a matter of common observation that many groups function best, or even only function at all, when the members are united against something outside the group, some other group or idea or practice. It is often said that there is nothing which unites people so easily and quickly as a common enemy. In times of war, or difficulty, the nation, as does the family, closes its ranks. Why should this be so? Firstly it points unmistakably to the existence of hostile feelings and tensions within the group itself, otherwise there would be no need to speak of 'closing the ranks'. Where these tensions cannot be safely handled inside the group they are most easily dealt with by projecting the anxiety and hostility arising from them outside. Other groups, or external circumstances generally, are then blamed for dissatisfactions having their origins within the group. This is often dangerous, it is usually morally unjustifiable, and in the long run it is always a weak solution psychologically. It is weak because by disposing of hostile feelings in this way a group tends to fail to come to grips with the whole of its problem, which is to attempt to canalize as large a proportion of its energies as possible in constructive efforts.

3   THE EXERCISE OF LEADERSHIP

Given a suitable common task, a group with a leader learns or fails to learn to work together almost wholly in terms of how leadership is exercised within it. What is the secret of leadership? It was Freud (1921) who gave us the essential clue. A leader is always in some respects a parent figure, in the sense that we tend to respond to him as we responded to our parents in the past. We tend to identify with him as we did with one or both of them. A group is thus united through a common identification with the leader and this is the primary source of authority, which although actually external, is through unconscious identification felt to be internal to each member. Thus in his exercise of leadership he relieves each of us of sole reliance on our own separate internal authorities. He is felt to carry a major responsibility for the behaviour of the group and becomes the repository of the 'group conscience'. Within this unity, individual affection and hostility between group members is subordinated to the common tie with the leader and within a well-knit group there can thus be experienced a sense of security which may only rarely be attained outside it.

Yet all is not peace and amity within the group—it is a matter of degree, of the dominant feelings called forth by the leader. Attitudes of affection, fear, rivalry and hostility which we first experienced in relation to our parents are automatically in some degree transferred to those who act as leaders in our groups. Our parents provided security, or failed to do so, inducing fear; they called out love or hate, and hate leads to fear and guilt. When they accepted and forgave our hostile acts, they removed the burden of our transgressions, our feelings of guilt, and thereby bound us ever more closely to them. So it may be with the leader.

Depending partly on the personal experience of group members and partly on how he exercises his leadership, the leader may in varying degrees be revered and also feared, or he may represent the respected but safe and approachable parent with whom we can talk openly and can even criticize, or he may appear as a weak figure whom we ignore, or a figure both weak and arbitrary against whom we openly or covertly rebel.

We are now in a position to understand the results of experiments into group climates and different forms of leadership. An authoritarian leader is a strong one in conventional terms and he may also be loved. When this happens identification with him is likely to be strong and to contain much primitive feeling. The group will follow him anywhere and he will not be criticized, both from fear of reprisals and because to criticize him is to criticize the group itself. He too is identified with the group, and there may be a state of complete mutual dependence and approbation. 'L'état c'est moi,' he says, and the group may also feel 'nous sommes l'état'. Such a group is powerful and may be very effective, within limits. Its members believe absolutely in its aims and its leader. Collectively the members may come to believe they have a divine mission, even when their purposes are diabolical. Such a group can thus safely commit the most terrible atrocities because the all-forgiving father is there to absolve communal and individual guilt. From this it may be seen that charismatic leadership is only a special case, in which the leader's own personality, the group membership and the circumstances of the time all combine to augment primitive unconscious feeling to the degree necessary for semi-mystical states to be experienced and for 'divine' forces to make their appearance. It is a fact, unfortunately, that it can be a very exhilarating experience to be a member of such a group, but only for part of the time and not indefinitely. Tension inside such a group is high, too high for ultimate safety; nemesis awaits it. The demand for complete obedience always tends to raise resentment and hostility. The leader is feared and hated as well as loved, precisely as children will fear and hate parents who will allow them no real individuality. For this reason the leader also fears the group. If these feelings were to be expressed too openly or too often within the group or toward the leader, this would endanger its existence and his. Therefore safety has to be sought in external aggression. The authoritarian leader feels this intuitively and is apt to seek or provide an external enemy, a scapegoat on whom the group can in fact avenge itself for the internal indignities which it has had to suffer. A certain amount of internal aggression too is almost always found, complete common identification with the leader not being in fact achieved; hence individual or factional rivalry, denunciations, betrayals and purges. In a mild, or even sometimes in a severe degree, all these phenomena can be found in authoritarian class-rooms. Even when outward order reigns peace has been bought at a high price. Group members in identifying with the leader tend to surrender their own internal authority to his, and with it their initiative and capacity for judgement. Learning therefore tends to be passive and merely absorptive, instead of active and creative. .

Weak or arbitrary leadership on the other hand is likely to be ineffectual in helping a group to learn to work together. Such leadership is unable to guarantee security and provide the focus for the evolution of an acceptable common purpose, because no effective identification with the leader is made, and/or because inconsistent use of authority leads to insecurity and heightens fear and resentment. Disruptive tendencies are at once apparent and both aggression and apathy appear. Moreover little or no use can be made of the collective experience and skill of the members, since there is little effective communication among them or between them and the leader.

This account is of course in many ways an over-simplification of group situations. Rivalry for the leadership role and rivalry for the exclusive attention of the leader are in fact common features. Moreover the inter-relation of group members among themselves permits of many additional complications. A more complete account would show how leadership roles may be divided and shared depending on the situation and how under suitable circumstances group members may come to have a clearer realization of the unconscious as well as the conscious dimensions of their relationship with the leader and each other. To the extent that this can happen, group activity can become more rational and less governed by unconscious factors. The good leader is usually able, even if only purely intuitively, to move in this direction. For a more fundamental and detailed analysis of group experience recourse should be had to Bion's work (1961).

From all this it is clear that what we might call optimum leadership is something qualitatively different from either authoritarian or weak leadership. It is not a matter of more or less authority at all, but of the qualities of relationship existing within the group. In such a group, identification with the leader is positive but relatively mild. In his turn the leader is not wholly identified with the group, but rather is both separate from it and a member of it. By virtue of this he can guide without domination, because the group is not afraid of him and he is not afraid of the group. Rather he loves the group in the sense of being concerned about its welfare as something quite distinct from himself. The parallel of course is with the good parent who loves and is concerned for his children, not as instruments for his own greater glory, or as minor editions of himself, but as separate growing beings each with a personal identity and destiny of his own. In this essential concern for others, not in dominance, lies the secret of the 'good' leader's group cohesive power. Because of this concern he is trusted, although not exempt from criticism. Nevertheless as well as concern, he must possess competence, i.e. knowledge and skill relevant to the common task. Thus at one and the same time he can be a reliable source of authority when it is needed, permissive and tolerant in his attitude toward experiment and exploration, participant in his activity, and respected for the knowledge and skill he can contribute. In the atmosphere sometimes described as 'democratic' which such a leader can create, aggression and apathy are diminished—although not necessarily eliminated—and productivity, satisfaction and personal growth are promoted.

This type of leader shows his concern and competence in practical ways by endeavouring to elicit the maximum contribution from each member, if need be by restraining the dominant, and encouraging the timid. He favours members learning from and helping each other, and expects to learn from them himself. Because of their identification with him the group is able to learn from him and to learn to be like him in the essential virtues of concern for and tolerance of others. It is in learning these attitudes and ways of behaving that the group learns to work together. This is the essence of the answer to our question of how a group learns to work together. It does so by internalizing in each member some of the concern and the competence of an effective leader with whom it has worked. This is central, other factors although important are subsidiary and for the most part consequential. Eventually, and if the group contains enough mature people, it can dispense with the leader's services, *qua* leader, if not entirely, then for long periods. The functions of the leader have then been appropriated by the group itself, that is, the values for which he stands have been effectively and securely internalized in each of the members. While leaderless groups may sometimes be a misnomer, the fact that friendship groups function effectively without any formal leadership or hierarchic structure, is a standing demonstration that human beings are, in principle, capable of attaining interpersonal relations sufficiently mature to dispense with the need for constant supervision by an externalized authority. The question whether a group can ever really be leaderless and still function, is I think a semantic one. Where the leadership function is sufficiently widely shared a limiting case can be reached in which it is a matter of convenience to refer to the situation as leaderless. Similarly if a group internalizes in phantasy the image of a 'divine' person and members respond to what are felt to be his wishes, it is reasonable to designate such a situation as 'leaderless' in the ordinary sense. Self trust, and its correlative mutual trust, can overcome inner anxiety and its correlative mutual fear. Ultimately and ideally, the aim of leadership should be the same as that often postulated for the State, and usually suggested for parental protection, namely that the need for it should diminish and even, ultimately, wither away.

Educational Implications

It should not be difficult to draw important educational implications from all this. Many such implications have already been drawn and have been put into practice. The appropriate use of group work (and sometimes, alas, its inappropriate use) is now the order of the day in many parts of our educational system. Yet it is clear that large areas remain unaffected still, and that even where group work is appropriately used, much still remains to be learned by many of us about creating optimum learning and working conditions for groups of children, of students and of teachers in schools and colleges.

How important to the teacher practitioner is a theoretical knowledge of group psychology? I myself maintain that it is not essential but that some acquaintance with it is very desirable. Many teachers are in themselves group cohesive personalities—some, alas, are not. But whatever our gifts, they can usually be enhanced by appropriate study both practical and theoretical. Practical experience of learning in groups under competent leaders is, however, essential for further progress. There is, therefore, at present a great need for the spread of insightful group work in teacher training itself. Without such experience forming part of their own education young teachers are not fully equipped to carry out effective group work with children. For students in training or for practising teachers, lectures on group psychology (like this one) can do little except to initiate what may be profitable reflections. It is only through practical experience that such reflection can be matured and fashioned into effective attitudes, habits of mind, and ways of behaving.

It is no accident that group work spreads principally by example and that the more fruitful experiments have been and are being carried out by people who have accepted the need for training. There is, however, a very wide range of effective ways of leading groups, and I would not here advocate any particular approach. It is true that experience of psycho-analytically oriented group work can be powerfully illuminating, but the methods used by the group leader in these situations do not provide in themselves an actual model of how to conduct groups in other, quite different circumstances, and without additional training and experience. Such techniques may be transferred to other settings with appropriate safeguards, as shown by the studies of Kitson (1962) and those of Herbert and Richardson already referred to, but it is generally speaking more relevant to seek the application of such a training experience in terms of increased insight into more conventional group procedures as has been brilliantly demonstrated by Michael Balint (1957) and by M. L. Johnson Abercrombie (1960). On the other hand, many people of diverse practical and theoretical outlooks have initiated and supported the use of group techniques in creative work with adults as well as children (Hourd 1961) and also in the structuring and management of national and international conferences by the New Education Fellowship (Morris, 1954; Tibble, 1956), the World Health Organization and other bodies.

Whatever the theoretical model used, the basic insights remain the same. There has to be a common task to the formulation of which members have themselves contributed. On the part of the leader there has to be a readiness to accept contributions from whatever source and to encourage all to make what contribution they can. He must display an evident and felt concern for all members of the group equally and for the progress of the group as a whole. In all sincerity and in true humility, he must be the servant of the group. To discharge such a task the leader needs to be sufficiently secure in himself to accept hostility when it comes, to have at least some natural insight into his own motives, and to be able to resist the blandishments of those members who wish to secure a special relationship to him at the expense of others. Above all he must be a good listener and observer. While recognizing the importance of language he must learn to detect 'the music behind the words', i.e. the latent dimension of feeling entering into all behaviour. He must rely for his authority upon his evident concern and competence, although his very competence sets a trap for him, if he is tempted into misusing it to impress his superiority upon the group.

In practice, helping a group to learn to work together may involve the preparation of special material and the contriving of suitable physical conditions, but in the last resort the leader's (and the teacher's) main instrument is simply himself—his own personality. Specific techniques are quite secondary and the use of gimmicks is not only fatal but a betrayal of trust. The road to success in group work lies in an increasing sensitivity to the inwardness of personal relationships. You may be tempted to think that the picture I have drawn of optimum leadership is one calling for a genius or a god for its realization. Not at all. It represents only what we mean by the activity of the good teacher and thus represents what we all, at times, achieve in some degree, and what we may all hold up before ourselves, as an ideal toward which we may continually strive.

References

ABERCROMBIE, M. L. JOHNSON, 1960. *The Anatomy of Judgment* (Hutchinson).

BALINT, M., 1957. *The Doctor, His Patient and the Illness* (Pitman).

BION, RICKMAN, FOULKES, BRIDGER and others, 1946. Bulletin of the Meninger Clinic, Vol. 10, No. 3.

BION, W. R., 1963. *Experiences in Groups* (Tavistock).

FOULKES and ANTHONY, 1957. *Group Psychotherapy* (Penguin).

FREUD, S., 1921. Group Psychology and the Analysis of the Ego. (Complete Works Standard English Edition, Vol. XVIII.)

GUNTRIP, H., 1961. *Personality Structure and Human Interaction* (Hogarth).

HERBERT, E. L., 1961. The Use of Group Techniques in the Training of Teachers. *Human Relations*, Vol. 14, No. 3.

HOMANS, G. C., 1951. *The Human Group* (Routledge & Kegan Paul).

HOURD, M. L., 1961. Some Reflections on the Significance of Group Work. *New Era in Home and School*, Vol. 42, No. 1.

JAQUES, E., 1951. *The Changing Culture of a Factory* (Tavistock).

KITSON, G. M., 1962. Group Methods and Their Relevance to Teacher Training. M. Ed. Thesis Leicester University.

LEWIN, K., 1947–48. (*a*) 1947 Group Decision and Social Change: in Newcomb, Hartley and others (Edit.). Readings in Social Psychology (Henry Holt).
(*b*) 1947 Frontiers in Group Dynamics, *Human Relations*, Vol. 1, Nos. 1 and 2.
(*c*) 1948, *Resolving Social Conflicts* (Harper).

See also:

LEWIN, 1939. Field Theory and Experiment in Social Psychology. *Amer. J. Sociol.* 44.

CARTWRIGHT and ZANDER, 1953. *Group Dynamics: Research and Theory.* (Tavistock) for authoritative summary of work of Lewin and his students.

LIPPETT and WHITE, 1943. The Social Climate of Children's Groups: in Barker, Kounin and Wright—*Child Behaviour and Development* (McGraw-Hill).

MENZIES, I. E. P., 1960. A Case Study in the Functioning of Social Systems as a Defence Against Anxiety: A Report on the Study of the Nursing Service of a General Hospital. *Human Relations,* Vol. 13, No. 2.

MORENO, J. L., 1934. *Who Shall Survive?* (Nervous Disease Publishing Coy.).

MORRIS, B. S., 1954. Chairman's Comment. *New Era in Home and School,* Vol. 35, No. 1.

RICE, A. K., 1963. *The Enterprise and Its Environment* (Tavistock).

RICHARDSON, J. E., 1951. (*a*) An Experiment in Group Methods of Teaching English Composition: in *Studies in Social Psychology of Adolescence* (Routledge).
(*b*) 1963. Teacher-pupil relationships as explored and rehearsed in an experimental tutorial group. *New Era in Home and School.* Vol. 44, Nos. 6 and 7.

RIESMANN, D., 1953. *The Lonely Crowd* (Doubleday).

ROBBINS, L., 1963. *Higher Education* (H.M.S.O.).

SPROTT, W. J. H., 1958. *Human Groups* (Penguin).

TAVISTOCK, 1946–47. (*a*) SUTHERLAND, J. D. Social Therapy: A Trend in Social Science. *Personnel Management,* Summer, 1946.
(*b*) WILSON, A. T. M. and others. Group Techniques in a Transitional Community. *Lancet,* 31st May, 1947.
(*c*) MORRIS, B. S. Education and Human Relations: in Jaques (Edit.) Social Therapy. *Journal of Social Issues,* Vol. III, No. 2, 1947.

TIBBLE, J. W., 1956. Conference Story (New Education Fellowship). See also: *New Era in Home and School*, Vol. 37, No. 10.

TRIST and SOFER, 1959. *Explorations in Group Relations* (Leicester University Press).

6

WILLIAM TAYLOR

Learning to live with neighbours

I

How and why do we learn—more particularly, how and why do we learn to live with neighbours? The 'why' is easier than the 'how'. The most dependent and helpless of the mammals at birth, we slowly and painfully learn the means by which our physical and material environment may be controlled and made orderly. But however sophisticated our control in these directions, we retain a large measure of social dependence. On the national and international level, the requirement that if we are to live at all we must learn to live together is beginning to impose its own ethic of co-existence. Domestically and in the many groups of which we are members, our need to be needed, our liking for being liked, the necessity for the approval of others if we are to develop and maintain a positive self-image, all combine to ensure our concern for the regard of our fellow creature, and give us the reciprocal obligation to provide an approving climate for others. To show how we become aware of the needs and responses of our neighbours, to trace the processes by which the individual is 'socialized' within the pattern of norms and standards, habits and traditions that characterize the society in which he lives and the groups of which he is a member—to do full justice to this theme would require far more than the space that I have at my disposal. I have chosen, therefore, to concentrate my attention upon the way in which our membership of educational groups—as teachers, pupils and students—influences the way in which we learn to live with each other.

In the course of what I have to say I shall be giving some attention to the experimental group study that has become a feature of the work of social psychologists in this country and the United States during recent years, and which Professor Morris has already referred to in his earlier lecture in this series. This experimental study exemplifies the processes by which group members learn to relate to one another, acquire the norms of the group, become aware of the ways in which they are responding to group pressures, and communicate from person to person. Such experiments highlight what is happening all the time in our ordinary social intercourse, in our daily relationships with our fellows. Experimental groups may be deliberately placed in a social vacuum, without a history, without traditions, without a hierarchy of power, a chairman or even a purpose—save that of 'being a group'—but most of our everyday groups are clearly not like this. Most of them exist within some kind of institutional framework, from which they take their form and shape. The school class, the work group and the leisure group are all artefacts of a set of institutional arrangements. If we designed school buildings differently, if we altered the shape and distribution of classroom furniture, if we mixed up children of different ages and levels of ability, we should find that the group we call a 'class' or 'form' would be very different from that typical of schools that are architecturally and organizationally more conventional. If most of our learning takes place within groups that are structured in accordance with certain principles of organizational arrangement, then it clearly behoves us to pay some attention to these if we are to understand how the groups work and the nature and quality of the learning experiences that membership of them involves. In this lecture, therefore, I am concerned with the way in which we learn from neighbours in the institutional rather than the individual context—if we must categorize, my point of view is that of the sociologist rather than of the psychologist. After a preliminary glance at the process of socialization within the early family environment, it is my intention to examine the external and internal patterns of relationship of the school, and to suggest some of the ways in which we could improve the quantity and the quality of the social learning that goes on in schools.

II

It is clear that the earliest and the most important proto-types of the child's later social relationships are laid down within the family. From the blooming buzzing confusion that allegedly characterizes the world of the young baby, there begin to be singled out certain aspects of the environment that respond to demand, that provide satisfaction of need. We have become familiar with the view that the relationship with the mother at this stage remains of vital importance as a pattern for other social relationships later in life.

It is not long before the child begins to recognize that he must adjust his demands to those of others if he is to preserve their goodwill and approval. The expectations of parents and siblings must be taken into account if the relationship with them is to be maintained, if, in Homan's terms, a balance of reward over cost is to be established. The capacity for compromise that this requires develops slowly and unevenly; the child's propensity for giving way on what parents might regard as the important issues, and digging his toes in on something that in their eyes seems tiny, trivial and unimportant, is well known as a source of bewilderment and tension within the family.

By four or five the willingness and ability to put the continuance of a social relationship above the pursuit of individual self-interest is quite well developed. The following dialogue took place between two sisters, one five, the other three, when playing with their dolls. It provides an example of how compromise can be achieved without loss of face, without completely surrendering the original position.

A (5 yrs.) The baby is asleep now.
B (3 yrs.) No, she's not, she's making a lot of noise.
A   No, she's fast asleep now.
B   Well, she's making a snoring noise through her nose.
A   Yes, just a little snoring noise.
B   But she'll be quiet soon.
A   Yes.

It is clear that the willingness to concede a point, to modify a position, will be greater when the environment is supportive and positive, when no dangerous risk to the integrity of the personality is involved in giving way. Without such an environment, compromise is seen as a form of surrender, agreement can only be in terms of something other than that originally desired by any single participant. The Father, in Strindberg's play of that name, disagrees with his wife regarding the residence of their daughter.

Laura   But supposing the father and mother were to decide things together?
Captain But how would that work out? I want her to live in town; you want her to live at home. The mathematical mean would be for her to stop at the railway station midway between home and town. You see? It's a deadlock![1]

If compromise is not to be seen as defeat, if agreement is to be a positive accomplishment rather than a negative concession, then the environment within which differences are adjusted must provide a sense of security, involve no deep sense of threat; such a setting must be furnished by the early family environment if foundations are to be laid on which positive social sentiments can later be built up.

[1] Strindberg, The Father in *Six Plays of Strindberg* trans. Elizabeth Sprigge, Doubleday Anchor, 1955, p. 16.

III

Beginning school results in an enormous extension of the range of 'significant others'. The child's awareness of self is inevitably enlarged by his association with more children, from different backgrounds and sometimes of different ages. In order to communicate with them, to receive reward and to minimize the costs of this association, he must learn the capacity to look at himself via the eyes of his friends, associates and teachers, to objectify his own individuality. In order to possess genuinely positive feelings towards others, that are not characterized by excessive dependence or neurotic anxiety, the child must possess a positive self-image. We cannot like others unless we like ourselves; we cannot avoid projection of our own negative impulses on to the motives of others unless we are willing to recognize these as part of ourselves, and to come to terms with them. The self-image is essentially a social product; it takes its shape from the pattern of relationships that we experience in the groups of which we are members; and, as I have suggested, the relationships thus developed are strongly influenced by the institutional settings within which the groups function. The family provides the first and most important pattern of relationships on which the child can model his responses; the school provides the second. Let us look, therefore, at the institutional setting of the school and examine the models that this provides for the process of learning to live with neighbours.

On the broadest front, the relationships of the school and its teachers with the individuals and groups that make up the neighbourhood served by the school must provide certain important learning experiences for children. It would, I think, be generally accepted that in England these take a different form from those characteristic of other English-speaking countries, particularly the United States and Canada. There, the tradition of the expanding frontier, the construction of the 'little red school house' as one of the first buildings of the new settlements, the absence of centralized control over education by church or state, have all encouraged a degree of community involvement in school affairs that contrasts sharply with the situation in this country. Here, because of the way in which the school system developed, its slow expansion to meet the educational requirements of the mass of the population in a manner largely determined by ruling *élites*, the involvement of the church, and the type of multi-purpose authorities that control education at the local level, the school is to some extent isolated from the community.[1] As a result, the teacher enjoys a degree of freedom from parochial influence that would be the envy of some of his harassed American colleagues. Such protection, however, is double edged. On the one hand it prevents the development of political, social or religious McCarthyism. On the other hand it shields the inefficient school from public criticism, and places all the initiative for the development of school and community contacts in the hands of the teachers—more particularly, the head teachers. In many areas, teachers have fully accepted the responsibilities thus laid upon them; flourishing parent-teacher associations build swimming pools, buy additional equipment, and support school journeys; the schools involve themselves in community affairs, helping old people, assisting in local hospitals, making and repairing toys for invalid children and so on. But such relationships are as yet scarcely typical of the educational scene as a whole. In the work of some parent-teacher associations the fact that this is a 'company union' is made all too clear; it is not unknown for an association to be dissolved unilaterally by a head teacher when it is felt to be 'going too far'. Relationships are probably easier in the suburbs than in the slum and problem areas. But difficulties are not restricted to such areas. Jackson and Marsden have shown the extent of

[1] For a discussion of this point see Baron G. and Tropp A., Teachers in England and America in *Education, Economy and Society*, ed. Floud, J. E., Halsey, A. H. and Anderson, C. A., Free Press, Glencoe, 1961.

the gap of misunderstanding and misinformation that can exist between the grammar school and working-class parents —basically anxious, co-operative parents most of them, very much concerned about finding ways in which they can understand what is being done for and to their children, but frustrated by inadequacies in the existing channels of communication and the absence of a common vocabulary with the school and all it represents.[1] And on the side of the secondary modern school, J. B. Mays has written vividly on the contrast between the culture and values represented by the school and the slum home. Describing an impressive performance of an excerpt from *The Wind in the Willows* he refers to the way in which such a display appears alien and out of context when compared with the type of social background from which the children come:

'How many of these older girls, dressed in their uniforms during the day, don tight-fitting skirts and go out jiving in the evening and what do they think then of country dancing and songs about cuckoos and Linden Leas? How many indeed know what a Linden Lea is and have seen one or heard the call of the cuckoo in real life?'[2]

There is implied in such studies the need for closer contact between the school and the home, for a greater effort to be made to minimize conflict, where it exists, between parents and teachers, to bring the school and the neighbourhood into a more fruitful reciprocal relationship.

It is clear that concern with these problems is going to increase in the next few years, and two points may be mentioned that are relevant in this respect. Parents have recently begun to organize in their own right, to form local associations and committees that are engaging in research, putting up candidates for local office, campaigning for better conditions in the schools. This has been made possible—and this is my second

[1] Jackson, B. and Marsden, D. *Education and the Working Class*. Routledge and Kegan Paul, London, 1962.
[2] Mays, J. B. *Education and the Urban Child*, Liverpool University Press, 1962, p. 90.

point—by the steadily rising educational standards of the mass of the population. Parents are beginning to take an interest in the schools that draws upon an increasingly coherent set of expectations as to what the teachers should provide, an increasingly informed appraisal of what can and should be done. Teachers must learn to work with the grain of these developments if they are to assist in the growth of neighbourly relationships in the communities they serve. This will not always be easy. Parents are often suspicious, aggressive and demanding, jealously protective of their own; despite recent changes, there is also a good deal of apathy, a too ready willingness to slough off family responsibilities on to the teachers. But if all this is true, it is equally true that the schools are not free from fault. An indifference to the difficulties of the home, a defensiveness and lack of open friendliness, a retreat into some kind of professional mystique that can be intimidating and frustrating to the outsider—all these can be found in some areas. How often in the end of the term report is one content to rely upon innocuous statements that give no offence but convey little information. My favourite is, 'He is working to the limits of his capacity.' What a wealth of disguised meaning there is in that phrase!

But some of the difficulties that may arise in trying to create better relationships between school and community are due to more fundamental factors than those I have already mentioned, and I would like to refer briefly to three of these. In the first place, the role of parent and that of teacher must be quite sharply distinguished in terms of the socialization function that they perform. The family is perhaps the most selfish unit of society. At heart, however generalized their ostensible concern with what goes on in schools, parents are involved in the protection and furtherance of the interests of their own children. Against this, the teacher must range herself on the side of universal justice, abhorring favourites, seeking to reduce rather than intensify the differences in the social and familial advantages of her pupils. In the relationships between parent and teacher, therefore, there must always be this residual element of conflict, which can only be accommodated, never completely eliminated. There are other bases for conflict in the relationship. The school is concerned always with raising the educational, cultural and social standards of its pupils, and, by implication, those of the neighbourhood. There may not always be adequate recognition of the legitimacy of the schools' activities in these directions. The school is *often* concerned with weaning the child from the standards of home and neighbourhood, with promoting some degree of social mobility which may be outwardly supported but inwardly resented; it is *always* involved with the development and maturation of children as separate individuals, in facilitating the process by which they grow away from their dependent status and acquire the opportunities to develop apart from the early family environment.[1] Finally, we should not be too hopeful that the opening up of better channels of communication between parents and teachers, school and community, the elimination of misunderstandings and the provision of more information, will *necessarily* lead to consensus, the reduction of conflict, an increase in positive feeling. Where genuine conflicts of interest exist, such a clearing of the ground can result in co-operation disappearing altogether; such co-operation as exists at present may in fact be dependent upon the very misunderstandings of aim and purpose that it has been suggested we should eliminate. The functional role of misunderstanding in facilitating relationships within complex social structures must not be ignored.

Such considerations should not perhaps deter us from making a necessary effort to increase parental understanding and to involve the school more closely in the life of its neighbourhood, but they may caution us against a too facile optimism about the ease with which this can be done.[2]

[1] See Parsons, T., The School Class as a Social System in *Education, Economy and Society*, op. cit.

[2] See Rex, J., *Key Problems of Sociological Theory*. Routledge and Kegan Paul, London, 1961, esp. Chapter VII.

IV

If the relationship between the school and the neighbour-hood provides one set of models from which children learn, it can be suggested that the pattern of relationships *within* the school itself exerts an even greater influence on the way in which the child comes to relate to the others of his environ-ment. As schools become larger, children of secondary school age stay on longer, and new forms of school organization are tried, there will be opportunities to reconsider the traditional pattern of relationships between teachers and pupils. At present there exist few systematic studies of the way in which schools function as social groups. As Ottaway has said, 'One has the feeling that nobody knows what goes on in schools, not even those who work in them, and least of all those who live and work in them. It needs an outside observer; it needs the anthropologist visiting the savage tribe.'[1]

There is nothing in the educational world corresponding to the intensive study of industrial organizations that has been carried on by sociologists and psychologists during the past thirty years. Yet there would seem to be plenty of scope for an increased concern with studies of organization and relation-ships within the school. Rudd and Wiseman made a study of the dissatisfactions of young teachers, and found that 'the irritations reported by this group of subjects made clear that feelings of dissatisfaction would not have been banished by increased public expenditure on salaries, buildings or reduc-ing the size of classes. Apparently, however, much benefit could accrue at little, if any cost, through the improvement of human relations in schools.'[2] From other reports by young

[1] Ottaway, A. K. C., The Aims and Scope of Educational Sociology, *Educational Review*, Birmingham, June 1960.

[2] Rudd, W. G. A. and Wiseman, S., Sources of dissatisfaction among a group of teachers, *British Journal of Educational Psychology*, XXX: 3. November 1962, p. 291.

teachers in their first appointments one knows that many schools do not provide the type of group support that enables the individual to express his feelings of doubt, hostility and excitement. The way in which our schools are at present organized tends to isolate the teacher behind the classroom door, to limit the extent to which his really significant role performances can be observed and evaluated by his colleagues, and to highlight other more observable but less educationally important aspects of these performances. Too frequently, the satisfaction of what might be called certain 'minimum task needs', such as quiet classes, a clean register and conscientiously marked exercise books, and, in the primary school, 'bright classroom walls', are the only accessible and observable symbols of satisfactory performance.

In the small school it is easier for teachers to function as a closely knit face to face group than for the staff of fifty or a hundred or more that will be increasingly characteristic of our large urban schools. The potential strains and interpersonal difficulties of the large institution are inevitably more serious and damaging than those of the small, where conflict must be resolved, differences must be reconciled, if the group is to continue to function at all. The head teacher of the large school of the future will need a more consciously developed skill in human relationships than his predecessor. I am by no means sure that we have given adequate recognition to this in our policy of training, selecting and appointing senior staff.[1]

There are other aspects of the way in which schools are organized that are relevant to our theme. In the past we have been too ready to rely upon 'purely educational factors', on amendments to the curriculum, reforms in teaching methods, to bring about a change in attitudes within the school, to encourage co-operation rather than competition, to enhance the children's sense of social responsibility. The effect of internal organizational factors on curricula change and

[1] Taylor, W., Training for Headship, *Forum*, Autumn, 1963.

social attitudes has been neglected. I would like to consider the nature of the influence that such factors can exert.

V

The social structure of most schools in this country is still strongly authoritarian. The English tradition invests the head with a form of charismatic authority quite unlike that of many of his European or North American counterparts.[1] Especially in secondary schools, the educational unit is still the class or form, and the very lay-out of rooms and desks facilitates and encourages a rather formal style of teaching in which the roles of teacher and pupil are kept separate and distinct. The comparatively recent realization that the architect and interior designer can do as much as the educationalist to determine what types of work the school will undertake is welcome as a pointer to future developments.

The formal classroom setting, the absence of suitable work spaces, do not encourage free group and individual work. The standards of personal behaviour which the authoritarian pattern demands are best secured by a formal classroom atmosphere, by chalk and talk and question and answer routines in which the respective roles of teachers and pupils remain at all times clearly defined and unambiguous. This clarity of role definition, avoiding the possible confusions and difficulties that a freer situation might involve, is welcomed by many teachers, especially when they are inexperienced or are dealing with adolescents, whose reactions and responses are less predictable than those of younger children and who raise more acute problems of control. The large number of roles that the teacher is asked to assume can often prove an embarrassment; expert, lawyer, policeman and judge, counsellor and friend—to fulfil all these roles without generating ambiguity and inconsistency is to ask a great deal. The role

[1] Stones, E., The Role of the Headteacher in English Education, *Forum*, autumn, 1963.

of 'expert' is perhaps the easiest to recognize and define, and there is a tendency on the part of many teachers to retreat within the protective frontiers of their subject, their discipline, a territory where only those who accept the rules may follow. Where divisions of age, interest and attitude exist and where social cohesion is based on some degree of compulsion rather than consent, the element of antagonism that is likely to result is dealt with most easily by structuring the whole situation as clearly and unambiguously as possible. The attitudes of teachers and head teachers in sometimes favouring a more systematic, academic and formal type of education than may be approved by educationalists and others not themselves immediately engaged in the schools, can be partly explained in terms of the internal needs generated by an authoritarian institutional structure. These constitute immediate and pressing influences on the decisions of practitioners, and their impact is not always perceived or understood by those outside the schools. Even individuals who have been engaged for some lengthy period of years in the classroom can undergo a rapid change of outlook once outside it, especially if a different set of institutional pressures, such as those of the university, the training college or the administrative office make themselves felt. The chief concern of the head and staff must be to maintain the school as a going concern, to find ways in which educational objectives can be fulfilled without undue strain, and to make do with whatever educational and social skills happen to be available. The process of seeking this equilibrium may encourage in some schools educational practices that run counter to the 'best opinion', to our understanding of what can or should be done in schools of this type and with children of the age and ability range concerned. But we cannot get schools to change in these directions by exhortation or appeal. What is necessary is to remedy the limitations of the organizational structure, to provide heads and teachers with the academic, administrative and social skills that will enable them to create new frameworks within which their work may be carried on, which will reduce the debilitating effect of interpersonal conflict and individual frustration, and encourage the staff to work together in terms of consciously determined objectives. To do this implies a much greater awareness on the part of the teachers of the patterns of human relationship within schools, and I would now like to consider some of the concepts and procedures within the field of human relationships study and training that are relevant to this purpose.

VI

Some of these concepts have become very familiar in recent years. The introduction of the teaching machine and programmed learning has given prominence to the notion of *feedback*, the means by which the individual is acquainted with the consequences of his actions and given opportunities to correct and to modify them. The principle is at work in systems of automatic control, where, for example, a thermostat responds to temperature changes and gives instructions to a heat source to switch on or off when the lower or upper limits of the range for which it has been set are reached. I have already suggested that the young child receives feedback from adults and from peers; their responses to his actions give him cues for his subsequent behaviour. To maintain a positive relationship with the significant others requires that he pleases them in his conduct, and he is therefore likely to inhibit his strongly egocentric impulses to grab, to kick or to scream in favour of more socially acceptable and socially rewarding actions. Whilst the mature adult has attained a greater degree of independence, he is still to a greater or lesser degree subject to group support and acceptance, and will frequently modify his behaviour to suit the norms of the group of which he is a member or the reference group to which he relates himself. In order to gain the approval of others he will mediate his behaviour in terms of what may be called 'performances'; consciously or unconsciously, he will play roles that are in accordance with certain patterns of group expectation.

The control that we achieve over the roles that we are playing, the degree of internal consistency that they possess, is often less complete than we would wish. The verbal component of our role-playing is sometimes belied by other behavioural elements. Goffman quotes the case of the Shetland Isle crofter's wife, who,

'. . . in serving native dishes to a visitor from the mainland . . . would listen with a polite smile to his polite claims of liking what he was eating; at the same time she would take note of the rapidity with which the visitor lifted his fork or spoon to his mouth, the eagerness with which he passed food into his mouth, and the gusto expressed in chewing the food, using these signs as a check on the stated feelings of the eater.'[1]

There is on the part of some a resistance to this type of analysis of basic social relationships, a tendency to contrast an awareness of all the subtleties that may be involved with the behaviour of the man who 'plays all his roles sincerely, in the sense of unreflective response to unscrutinized expectation'.[2] Such behaviour may be natural, but it is scarcely social; a decision on the part of the majority of mankind to behave in this way would soon lead to a complete breakdown in social relations. The important issues of principle that this approach to human relations *does* raise are related more to problems of conformity and independent behaviour, and I propose to say a little more about this in a moment. For the present, however, it is sufficient to note that if the individual is going to recognize the effects of his behaviour on others, if he is to possess a reliable self-image, he needs to be sensitive to feedback, and able to recognize, interpret and be sensitive to the human consequences of his actions. The notion of *sensiti-*

[1] Goffman, E., *The Presentation of the self in everyday life*, Doubleday Anchor, 1959, p. 7.

[2] Berger, P. L., *Invitation to Sociology*, Doubleday Anchor, New York, 1963, p. 152.

vity training is at the heart of many of the human relations programmes that are offered by universities and independent bodies in this country and abroad. Such training is provided in a variety of ways. It is clear that a person cannot be sensitized in the way that I have suggested by instruction or exhortation, no matter how persuasive the style of the lecturer or tutor concerned. The personality will usually resist the type of change that is required; the content of lectures will either be dismissed or reinterpreted in a way that will make it 'harmless'.

In our everyday discussions of how people learn to get along with each other, we frequently refer to the value of *experience* of a wide variety of social situations as the key to success. It follows that training programmes should endeavour to provide experiences of this kind; the student must be involved, cognitively and emotionally, in the process he is studying if he is to understand what it is all about and be capable of putting the lessons that he has learned into action. To this end, much of the training is carried out in experimental group settings. The unstructured training group, or 'T' group, is one of these. With the usual external and internal group controls missing, participants establish their own standards, norms and patterns of communication. Consultants attached to the group help to make members conscious of what is going on, and refer this to principles of group functioning that are discussed, in the lectures and seminars associated with the 'T-group' work. The group's own experience is thus used as a basis for its members' study of how interpersonal relationships develop in the face to face situation, and in the process participants can identify and understand their own reactions to authority and to colleagues, the nature of their dependency needs, the patterns of communication that are set up within the group, and the factors that determine the way in which individuals respond to group pressure.

The National Training Laboratories in the United States and the Tavistock Institute of Human Relationships in this country have pioneered group development courses which combine 'T' group with other forms of group work and the study of the sociological and psychological principles that underlie the way in which people learn to relate to one another. The Tavistock courses have been open not only to educationalists but also those from industry and commerce, hospital administration and other settings where human relationships are of decisive importance, and an increasing number of individuals are now benefiting from the training that they provide. In industry there has been a proliferation of personal relations learning techniques other than the conventional lecture and discussion methods, which are recognized as being of limited value in bringing about changes in attitude and behaviour. Case study, role playing, directed exercises and projects, business games, leadership simulations and many other devices are being used to develop a greater degree of sensitivity to human relations problems, more sophisticated skills for use in those situations which involve dealing with people.[1] The extension of these techniques to the educational field is proceeding very slowly. In the United States the Universities Council for Educational Administration has developed a complex simulation, based on in-basket techniques, which is used in connection with the in-service training of senior school staff. I have recently produced some experimental materials of this kind for use in this country, and these are being used in connection with courses for head and deputy head teachers.

VII

It would be wrong to suggest that there is uniform agreement as to the validity and usefulness of the techniques that I have described. Some people do not like the element of calculation that such training seems to introduce into social

[1] For a useful survey of current practice, see Hacon, R. J., *Management Training*, English Universities Press, London, 1961.

relationships. The same people sometimes seem to be nostalgic for the more direct and spontaneous patterns of relationship that they allege are characteristic of rural and urban working-class groups. It seems to me that such patterns only *appear* to be spontaneous and natural because the middle-class observer is in fact several jumps ahead in the relationship game; to the group participants themselves they may present just as many problems and difficulties as are typical of groups at other levels of society. Others reject the need for theoretical formulations in the area of human relationships. But, as MacGregor has stated. 'Theory and practice are inseparable. . . . It is possible to have more or less adequate theoretical assumptions; it is not possible to reach a managerial decision or to take a managerial action uninfluenced by assumptions, whether adequate or not. The insistence on being practical really means, 'Let's accept *my* theoretical assumptions without argument or test.'[1] More substantial objections are directed towards the philosophy that underlies much human relations work. Too great a dependency on a structural-functional analysis of society, the tendency to strive for consensus at almost any cost, the view that conflict is anomic and should be eliminated, evidence of inadequate interest in the instrumental, as compared with the socio-emotional tasks of leadership—all these are objections that deserve consideration, but which I can do no more than refer to in passing now.

The slow pace of development of human relations work in education can be partly accounted for by inertia, partly by the lack of demand, partly because of the misgivings of those who are mindful of the dangers of manipulation, critical of the assumptions that may lie behind what looks uncommonly like a policy of making friends and influencing people. Considerable misgivings have been expressed regarding developments in the United States, where it is alleged there has grown up a trend towards what Riesman has called 'false

[1] McGregor, D. M., *The Human Side of Enterprise*, McGraw Hill, London, 1960, p. 7.

personalization', the attachment of too great a significance to 'belongingness', to groupism in all its aspects. Associated with this trend is a view of educational and social change which puts its emphasis on adjustment and adaptation in group terms, on 'getting along with people' as almost the supreme virtue, on the paramount need for agreement, almost independently of the desirability or otherwise of what the group wants to do, of the purpose for which it exists, of the end towards which its agreement is a means. Perhaps it is because so many of the groups to which we belong are concerned with purposes that are apparently trivial, meaningless and remote that we need to concentrate attention upon process rather than purpose. These criticisms may do less than justice to the motives and methods of human relations practitioners, but they are an undoubted element in the misgivings that have been voiced regarding the wider employment of such techniques. The line between harmonizing personal relationships as part of a deliberate policy, using group skills and insights which are not available to those others concerned in the process, and manipulation, is a very narrow one.

The deeper anxieties of the critics of human relations programmes are directed towards the dangers of excessive conformity, the risks of caring so much about what our neighbours think of our actions that we uncritically adopt the standards of whatever group we happen to join. The factors making for conformity and non-conformity have been given a great deal of attention in recent years by psychologists and sociologists. In the United States, this has been coupled with the realization that American non-conformity is an ideology rather than a fact; in the words of Lionel Trilling, 'Admiring non-conformity and loving community, we have decided that we are all non-conformists together.'[1] Concern with this theme has extended to the educational world, and a number of studies have shown how students may be dominated by the values of the peer group at the expense of intellectual con-

[1] Lionel Trilling, *Freud and the Crisis of our Culture*, quoted by Jahoda, M., Conformity and Independence, *Human Relations*, 12: 1959, p. 99.

cerns, how the curriculum has tended to centre attention on social skills at the expense of rigorous academic study, how principles of adjustment, adaptation, integration and consensus have penetrated the training of teachers and diverted attention from the primary teaching role of the school.

Among the most percipient critics of such trends is David Riesman, whose *Lonely Crowd* has become something of a contemporary sociological classic. Riesman labels the tendency to conform to the perceived expectations of others as 'other direction'—'What is common to all the other-directed people is that their contemporaries are the source of direction for the individual—either those known to him or those with whom he is indirectly acquainted, through friends and through the mass media.'[1] Other-direction is associated, according to Riesman and those who have extended his analyses, with the type of bureaucratic, technological mass society in which we live. In former times the individual was isolated from the judgement of his peers to a greater extent than today; there existed little feedback regarding the nature of the self-image. Economic life was insecure, consumption less important than production, thrift was encouraged. The quality of the goods produced was more important than the social relationships associated with the process of production; risk taking was the way to success, and individual entrepreneurial judgement was highly valued. Today these conditions have changed. The individual leads a more varied social life, is a member of many groups, and in our pluralistic society can escape fairly easily from the restrictions and dissatisfactions that may be associated with some group situations to others which are more rewarding. There is a considerable measure of self-consciousness, and the self-image is well developed. The former stress on production has been replaced by the opportunity for more consumption—in fact, a high level of consumption has become essential for the health of the economy. Mass production has increased the im-

[1] Riesman, D., *The Lonely Crowd*, Yale University Press, New Haven, 1950, p. 21.

portance of a favourable social climate in the factory; strikes, disagreements, high levels of individual stress and frustration are all expensive; the ability to work alongside others without conflict and undue strain is an important element in the individual's work skills. Individual risk taking is no longer the path to success—wrong decisions have too serious consequences; we live in the age of the committee and the agreed decision.[1]

These are generalizations of the broadest kind, but most of us will recognize their validity as descriptions of certain types of change that have been taking place in some areas of our social and economic life during the past fifty years. Schools and pupils have not remained unaffected by these changes. Riesman has elsewhere criticized many secondary schools in the United States on the ground that they are giving many youngsters 'what amounts to a post-graduate education in social relations when what they most need is something very different, namely preparation for certain long-term intellectual and humanistic interests that are momentarily under pressure and apt to be squeezed out'.[2]

Coleman has documented the way in which high schools develop norms of scholastic effort that are as pervasive in their influence on pupils' output as the standards of the workers in the Hawthorn plant 'Bank Wiring Room'.

'The same process which occurs among prisoners in a jail and among workers in a factory is found among students in a school. The institution is different, but the demands are there, and the students develop a collective response to these demands. This response takes a similar form to that of workers in industry—holding down effort to a level which can be maintained by all. The students' name for the ratebuster is the 'curve-raiser' or the D.A.R.—the 'damned average raiser' and their methods of enforcing the work re-

[1] Kallen, D. J., Inner Direction, Other Direction and Social Integration setting, *Human Relations*, 16: 1 2/63, p. 75.

[2] Riesman, D., *Constraint and Variety in American Education*, University of Nebraska Press, 1956 (Doubleday Anchor Edition, 1960, p. 149).

stricting norms are similar to those of workers—ridicule kidding, exclusion from the group.'[1]

Martin Trow has examined the culture of the American college, and finds that the socially supportive student sub-cultures within these institutions, with their emphasis upon the friendly exchange of social sentiments and getting on with people, can help to insulate the student against the impact of his formal education, can encourage 'the continuous murmur, the continuous bull session (that) Malinowski called "phatic communion", essentially friendly noises by which one indicates that one is a member of the tribe and the kind of person one can get along with'.[2] On the basis of his own studies of American college life, Riesman concludes that 'research on higher education must confront the possibility . . . that loyalty to the ideal of individualistic excellence may be at odds with the unequivocal loyalty to the college, the state or the nation'.[3]

All this evidence on the dangers of too much emphasis upon the socializing aspects of education, on the ability to get on with others, cannot be ignored. I do not think, however, that it should deter us from greater efforts in the direction of harmonizing relationships in schools, colleges and elsewhere, of helping people to learn to live with neighbours. We have never developed in this country the type of concern with human relations that the American critics dislike. Courses with such titles as 'creative living' have never appeared in the syllabuses of our schools. Our counselling and guidance services are poorly developed and inadequate to meet obvious present-day needs. Our schools, as I have already tried to indicate, are still fundamentally authoritarian in structure and process. For all these reasons, there still exists plenty of

[1] Coleman, J. S., Academic Achievement and the Structure of Competition in *Education, Economy and Society*, op. cit., p. 379.

[2] Trow, M., Recruitment to College Teaching in *Education, Economy and Society*, op. cit., p. 614.

[3] Riesman, D., The Influence of Student Culture and Faculty Values in the American College in Ruitenbeck, H. M. (ed.) *Varieties of Modern Social Theory*, E. P. Dutton, New York, 1963, p. 328.

scope for improving human relationships within schools and for providing pupils with a more systematic social education, without necessarily imperilling intellectual and academic standards.

To understand how groups work, to be willing to respond to the needs and aspirations of others in the group, need not of itself foster a dangerous degree of group dependency, an excessive conformity, a fear and avoidance of all forms of conflict. To be sensitive to feedback, to receive and recognize information regarding the effects of our actions upon others, need not involve a slavish surrender to group opinion or group judgement. We can illustrate this with reference to the functioning of the thermostat that I referred to earlier. If we try to put the upper and lower limits of the range for which the instrument is set too close together, if we try to secure a completely steady temperature, the signals for switching off will coincide with those for switching on. To use an analogy, we can say that the thermostat has become too self-conscious, and as a result has lost its usefulness as a guide to action. If the thermostat is to work properly there must be a lag between the source of information and the source of action.

'This does not mean that the source of action must hesitate before it accepts the information. *It means that it must avoid identifying itself with the source of information.* We saw that when the furnace responds too closely to the thermostat, it cannot go ahead without also trying to stop, to stop without also trying to go ahead. This is just what happens to the human being, to the human mind, when the desire for certainty and security prompts identification between the mind and its source of information. It cannot let go of itself. It feels that it should not do what it is doing, and that it should do what it is not doing. It feels that it should not be what it is, but be what it isn't . . . the effort to remain always good or happy is like trying to hold the thermostat to a constant 70 degrees by making the lower limit the same as the upper.'[1] (Italics mine.)

[1] Watts, A. W., *The Way of Zen*, Thames and Hudson, 1957 (Penguin Books, 1962, p. 158).

All this is put in individual terms, but it is equally applicable to the behaviour of the group. We need to receive and respond to feedback, to see ourselves as others see us, but we must at the same time avoid identifying ourselves with the source of the information, avoid surrendering our individuality to the group. To do this does not mean eliminating our self-consciousness of social process, reducing the importance of sensitivity in human relationships, trying to act in 'natural' ways—we cannot do this in the world in which we live. What is needed is to be conscious of our own self-consciousness, to be aware of the ways in which we can be influenced by the groups of which we are members. As Riesman has put it, 'the autonomous man growing up under conditions that encourage self-consciousness can disentangle himself from the adjusted others only by a further move towards even greater self-consciousness'.[1] We cannot escape from the fact that the groups of which we are members influence our behaviour and our decisions. We *can* make ourselves aware of the processes by which this takes place, and thereby put ourselves in the position where we can retain our freedom of choice, where we can balance the comparative costs of group disapproval or personal disesteem. Without this individual point of reference, learning to live with neighbours can become a form of sophisticated 'group-manship', a process so other-directed as to lose all contact with the standards and principles on which behaviour is based, that lacks the 'investment in the issue' that Marie Jahoda sees as the basis of principled action.[2] To succeed in learning to live with one's neighbours is of little benefit if one can no longer live with oneself. Sensitivity to the needs and reactions of others is empty unless it is related to a set of firmly held standards of conduct and behaviour which constitute personally valid guides to action. We must be capable of receiving feedback not only from the ephemeral group situation of the moment, but also from our own understanding of how

[1] Riesman, D., *The Lonely Crowd*, op. cit., p. 259.
[2] Jahoda, M., Conformity and Dependence, op. cit.

the present problem is related to past events and future possibilities, from our individual knowledge, understanding and
commitment, our principles and our standards. Without
such impersonal feedback, without the strengthening of
individuality that is required, we learn to live with others
only on the basis of shared weakness, not of interdependent
strength.

VIII

What are the implications of all this for research and
action? First, it seems to me that schools need to pay far more
attention than at present to their relationships with the
neighbourhoods they serve. Without false optimism regarding the success that will attend such efforts, and mindful of
the need to resist those pressures from outside that devalue
and undermine the principles and standards that schools
should strive to maintain, there should be a greater attempt
than at present to involve community and parental skills and
resources in the work of the school, and the school in the life
of the community. Second, we need far more information
than is at present available regarding the impact of the school
as an institution on the social values, habits and aspirations
of pupils. What we know and surmise about this at present
suggests that schools can influence the capacities of their
pupils to live with neighbours in several ways. The pattern of
their institutional arrangements can provide a model which
comprises a variety of elements of mutual goodwill or suspicion, fruitful co-operation or anomic competition, manifest
concern or interpersonal distrust. Official aims can be belied
by administrative actions—I am sometimes struck by the
contrast between the claims of schools on the subject of
'training for social responsibility' and what actually goes on
in them. To mention but one example, at the age of five
children are often allowed to make their own way into the
school buildings, to settle down to their work, to find new

things to do when they have finished the old. At the age of fifteen, after ten years' schooling, and a few months before being expected to behave in a responsible way in factory or office, many boys and girls are lining up in playgrounds at the blast of a whistle, prior to being escorted to their class-rooms through corridors patrolled by observant prefects. All kinds of administrative and safety factors can be advanced to justify such action, but it reflects but little credit on the success of the cumulative training in social responsibility that surely should have been provided during those ten years. Too often one feels that situations are merely being contained, rather than having their full possibilities for social education exploited. There is scope for experiments with team teaching and other techniques that replace the traditional *confrontation* of teacher and class that is still the basic procedure by means of which we interpret our educational purpose.

My third point regarding research and action follows from the second. It is impossible to repudiate the growing bureau-cratization of schools, the increasing importance of social as well as instrumental skills in the work of teacher and head. If size and complexity cannot be avoided, then their long-term consequences should be faced. We can no longer rely upon the charismatic influence of head teachers to create a situa-tion in which the effective pursuit of viable educational aims can be coupled with a positive and supportive social climate. The head teacher of the future will need a range of adminis-trative and social skills which 'experience' alone may not be capable of providing. There would seem to be scope for pro-viding some form of specific training for senior staff that recognizes the importance of this. Finally, we should give attention to the provision of a wider range of social skills in the curriculum. It is possible that the best way to do this is not to concentrate all our efforts on new hybrids, on inte-grated courses, on social studies and committee procedure—although such direct teaching undoubtedly has its place—but by ensuring that the contribution that literature, poetry, drama and history can make towards the development of social understanding and social skills is fully realized and implemented.

These may appear to be slender conclusions to our consideration of so broad a theme. More active involvement in the community, research on school organization, human relations training for senior staff, more attention to the social implications of what we teach. Compared with the vast problems of international agreement that confront us in the world today such proposals may seem trivial. Yet, with each generation, the task of learning to live with neighbours begins again in the family and the individual classroom. Nothing can be assumed; with each child born we begin the task anew; and to each child born there is something new to teach, some additional element of understanding and experience that was not there when the previous generation came into the world. Cumulatively, the tasks of the teacher and the school become more complex and difficult. In this situation, anything that can be done to facilitate and improve the quality of social learning that takes place within schools assumes importance. It is to be hoped that current developments in the organization and content of our educational provision will provide fresh opportunities for a proper significance to be attached to the recurring task of learning to live with neighbours.

PART TWO

7

RICHARD HOGGART

Learning to deal with mass persuasion

This is pre-eminently an age of persuasion. One sociologist has called it 'the consensus society' in which, through a great many interacting changes, almost everyone has 'entered' society, has reached the level at which they have to be persuaded to do things (and are financially worth the persuading) rather than to be ordered to do so. For all sorts of purposes, good, bad and indifferent, consent has to be obtained, or 'engineered' as they say now . . . by manufacturers or by governments; so as to increase the proportion of science undergraduates or to increase the wearing of crash helmets, and so on. All these activities need the same kind of scrutiny.

I have chosen to talk mainly about advertising because advertisements are obvious and known to everybody. But to concentrate too much on them can be a substitute for engagement with harder background issues. What is true of advertising is true of much political propaganda, of much charitable propaganda, and of much religious propaganda.

Nowadays, some teachers are making their practice more relevant to the cultural situation of their pupils. But they are still exceptions. Too many teachers, perhaps especially in grammar schools, wash their hands of the whole matter and operate as though they live within a closed classical world. Some do not find the issues real to them for an opposite reason: they are at home in the mental climate of the persuaders.

I believe that we should be involved, critically involved here. We ought to be better informed and more precise in analysis. We ought to acquire a better sense of the general case for and against mass persuasion. We ought to decide how we can best apply this knowledge to our practice as teachers. So I will spend most of my time looking at the justifications commonly made for advertising and restating the case against. After that I will briefly suggest lines which our practice as teachers might follow.

In laying out the defence of mass advertising I will describe the half-dozen or so arguments most commonly employed. It is argued, first, that advertising is an essential feature of the economy of an industrially advanced society. Available goods need to be known; how can they be known other than by public advertising over the length and breadth of the country? At this point defenders sometimes illustrate their text with a genteel eighteenth-century advertisement announcing that Mr. So-and-So of Cheapside-atte-Strande or some such pleasantly old-fashioned address offers fragrant Indian tea for the delectation of ladies and gentlemen. Further, they argue that advertising, through the process of filtration which the fierce interplay of competition and of national publicity causes, ensures that only good goods survive. They add that this makes for cheaper goods since the successful good goods can now be produced in larger quantities. This part of the defence concludes that the sheer survival —let alone the more agreeable working—of mass democracies demands advertising, the engineering of consent, all the time and at all levels.

The advertisers also claim that they fairly accurately represent 'ordinary folk'. Those who object to advertising are intellectual or emotional snobs, secretly despise ordinary people and are out of touch with them. Ordinary people, for their part, trust advertisers; so the contract is mutual.

Advertisers are 'sincere'; they have 'an acute sense of personal responsibility'; they must show 'common sense plus deep rich human understanding' or they will fail.

The apologists go on to say that advertising helps to teach us how to live in a changing society. When a society is socially as fluid as ours, when so many people are implicitly asking such questions as: what food do people in our position eat when they go out for a meal? how do our kind of people entertain their guests? where should our kind of people go for holidays? what kind of clothes should we wear? and so on, through hundreds of seemingly slight questions which indicate a search for style (but which are not slight because what is really being sought is a style of *life*)—in such a society, it is said, 'advertising may play a large part, perhaps a leading part, in teaching the art of living'.

The next defence contradicts the one above. Here, it is said that advertising has no—or practically no—effect, that people can 'see through it', and know if they are being 'got at'. But they don't feel indignation against advertising as its critics do; they rather enjoy it all, whether they are being politely wooed or jollied along with huckster's blarney. Indeed, much advertising is deliberately comic and parodies itself; and people appreciate this.

The next defence, like an earlier one, accepts the view that advertising does affect attitudes. But it assumes the effects are sometimes bad rather than good—and then disclaims prime responsibility. It says: even if we do have some ill effects, this is not our fault. We are reflectors, not prime movers; we have to take people as we find them. The blame can be laid—ironically, since they are among our chief critics—at the door of teachers. The education given in schools, and especially in secondary modern schools, does not sufficiently 'foster the critical faculty'. In fact, it actually 'encourages conformity'. Even if, the defenders continue, we do play on people's weaknesses, we are not the only sinners. We are bearers of guilt for other people, but are in fact less subtly guilty than most of these others. Most of us can keep our sins hidden; the advertisers are exposed in the market-place. After a while the advertiser begins to look, on this argument, rather *more* honest than most of us.

It follows, and this is the last main line of defence, that those who attack *are* humbugs. Perhaps, the tone sometimes suggests here, they have secret vices which they are trying to ignore by using the advertisers as scapegoats. Certainly they are 'puritan paternalists', 'moralists and aesthetes . . . arrogant autocrats . . . mystics moved by so-called cultural values'.

Against defences like these—and I have given only an out-line of the main approaches—how does one put the opposi-tion case? The first line of defence, you will remember, was based on economic need. I am not professionally competent to rebut this, but can register some serious qualifications. The first is that much of this case seems to be founded on pre-sumption. Economists differ about whether advertising re-duces the cost of goods; it has not been absolutely proved that in either the short or the long run advertising in itself ensures that good products drive out bad; nor has it been proved that the survival of a modern democracy depends on mass advertising; more, in all this the defenders are usually—by comfortable implication—defending straight informative ad-vertising, not that kind of advertising which is much more common . . . advertising which plays upon the emotions. The distinction between informative and emotional advertising is difficult, and this difficulty has given the defenders much scope for ambiguities. We can and should for practical pur-poses distinguish between largely informative advertising and advertising which moves out to play with increasing skill and obliquity on more and more complex and submerged emo-tional needs.

Since most advertising is of this kind the defence of adver-tising on economic grounds (even if it were more than a presumption) begins to look dubious. We find ourselves de-fending the use of bad means for 'respectable' ends. Some-times advertising's play on the emotions *is* thus defended—as inseparable from, and less important than, its benefits. You can't have the benefits of coal, we are told, without being prepared for slag heaps to spoil the landscape. But the analogy simply does not fit. If the burden of the 'subjective' case against advertising is accepted, we cannot so easily put it aside on the grounds of economic need and benefit. If we do, we are in an interesting semantic condition. We are saying: 'Advertising will help to bring about a better society. But yes, it will be a worse society. Still, you can only have a better society, so to speak, by being prepared for it to be worse.' By the existence of unresolved ambiguities such as these the practitioners can make the climate more favourable to their own activities. What they are really saying is that the good society (which they conflate with a society with a high level of physical conveniences and improvements) can *only* flower if it is bedded in the exploitation of weakness.

The next line of defence took the form of saying that advertisers were fair to ordinary people, and so were respected themselves. But we need only remember the men who take part in the detergent advertisements on commercial television, those men whose mouths crease as they smile at the housewives in their little council houses but whose eyes remain watchful, hard and lost. Or we may remember the drumming, banal, hard sell of some of the other commercials And we are bound to ask: 'How, if you treat people as such morons, can you be said to "respect" them?' and to add that paid-for public palliness is not affection (and that there is a difference between the kind of synthetic palliness we are describing here and the palliness of a variety comic); and finally to say that a phoney pal of this kind is more patronizing than an ordinary old-style class-snob.

So when the advertisers describe the public as 'intensely interesting, lovable and wholly unpredictable' we have to reply that a sentence like that *sounds* false and that the advertisers can't think we are quite as unpredictable as all that, or they'd soon be out of business. And when, with less cant, another advertiser says 'catch them young and catch them in the first flush of their financial independence', we have to say that that sounds not like 'love' but like straight manipulation. When they talk, yet again, about their accuracy in reflecting the tastes and qualities of ordinary people we must reply that they do not comprehensively represent those qualities. They address themselves to parts, to some of the more elementary or undeveloped qualities, to those aspects which are most likely to further their own ends.

Does advertising teach us how to live in a changing society? Certainly education of this kind—social education it is sometimes called, though there is more to it than that term suggests—education of this kind is mediated by all sorts of agencies. It is plainly going on extensively today. In times of particular social fluidity, social education (consciously or not) becomes a prime need. In a more open society more and more of us have to make more and more individual decisions, rather than follow the customs of our street or profession. Almost inevitably the established voices, the accustomed mediators, are slow in catching on; their tones are bound to seem old fashioned. The new socially educative voices are in their nature more freely floating and more 'contemporary'. They have a more accurate sense of the way choices are expressed, those choices each of which, as I've said before, may seem slight. ('Shall we buy these curtains? that kind of drink? that magazine? that opinion?') but which have important common roots, since they suggest a way of life in which we wish to feel secure.

Some researches do suggest that advertisers effectively sell, to some extent, their picture of the good life. What they mean by the good life, as we have seen, is a life whose assumptions have been taken over from the economic drives of the mass-production society itself: consumption as a good in itself, the urge to increase one's personal rating together with the acceptance of a bland gregariousness. So the process is circular. Thus, one of the dichotomies which have dogged men over the centuries—the quarrel between the good and the expedient—comes within sight of being solved. The good *is* the expedient. It therefore becomes harder but more necessary to say again that the question of 'how to live' begins with an assessment of the quality of life offered within a society, not in an adjustment to its assumptions.

In making this assessment flexibility of mind is of first importance. But again there is some evidence from researches that the persuasions of mass communication tend to make taste set at a level which represents a common denominator, and so work against flexibility. It may not matter if we are led to conform in our choice of motor-cars or butter. The process does matter when it touches ideas or the imaginative life.

We are urged to conform (within what look like reasonable limits and with some appearance of interesting available variations) in our choice of goods, and so we learn to conform in our tastes. There is an interesting 'feedback' here, according to some recent evidence. It suggests that in mass communications demand is largely a function of supply, that we like what we get, that the mass media help to create the taste by which they are enjoyed, that increasingly (if left alone) they write their own tickets. In these senses they are de-educators rather than educators towards the good life: they make more sparse the exercise of choice, they encourage the accepting of what is already offered; they reduce dissent to a permitted variation and so reduce the play of human will.

But according to another line of defence the media had *no* effect. We are told that, apart from a minute proportion of the really stupid, people see through the persuasions. If this is so, we can only ask again why the advertisers are wasting so much time in a fruitless exercise—and one which does seem pretty determined. But we can go further, using various pieces of evidence, and insist that far more people do believe, genuinely believe, what the advertisements tell them than the advertisers like to admit.

The Pilkington Committee on Broadcasting recommended that advertising magazines should be permitted. Naturally, the companies running these magazines did not like this proposal or the government's acceptance of it. One of them commissioned a survey to ascertain what people thought about advertising magazines. Were the actors putting over an advertiser's message or making a personal recommendation? The company seemed cheerful about the results: 'There seems little doubt that the vast majority are under no illusions as to what is happening in these advertising magazines.' The survey showed that of the viewers who had a definite opinion about the role of a performer—in this case Jimmy Hanley in *Jim's Inn*—28 per cent thought the products were actually used by him, 72 per cent thought he was giving the advertisers' sales points. Surely these are forbidding figures: practically 3 out of 10 literally deceived. One wonders when the television company would start getting worried. They seem to have been exploiting intellectual or educational inadequacy and the capacity for belief in almost a third of their viewers.

I have said that research does suggest that mass media has an effect on attitudes. It seems to be a triggering rather than a causative effect. They may not be prime causes of shifts in attitudes but seem able to reinforce existing predispositions, especially those which are found in the groups to which we belong. They make it less likely that we shall look outside. Also, the media seem able to feed on and extend, though only slowly, psychic disturbance; that is, to encourage the insecure, the delinquent and the neurotic in their insecurity, delinquency and neurosis. On both these grounds, whether in reinforcing existing attitudes among the more or less normal or in increasing disturbance among the already disturbed, the media have some effect on attitudes and values. Since life is difficult enough at any time and clarity only patchily attained it seems a pity to spend so much time in confusing things.

Another reply to this particular charge formed the next line of defence. Here we were told that education does not 'foster the critical faculty' and so 'encourages conformity'.

Coming from advertisers, this is certainly brass-necked; still, how far do we as teachers 'foster the critical faculty' and how far do we let conformity grow, at any rate by default? Trying to 'foster the critical faculty' is tiring and can disturb us as well as our pupils. So most of us do not do enough in this way. Again, we can encourage conformity not only by positive actions (few of us would do that) but by omission, by sticking to unexamined routines of behaviour in and out of class, or to tired assumptions about experience and purpose. I think much in our teaching is still implicitly conformist in these ways. You can't properly attack the mass persuaders in society if you have not asked questions about the nature of that society.

Still, we should refuse to be lumped with the advertisers as culprits charged jointly with failing to 'foster the critical faculty' and with encouraging conformity. We don't *aim* to reduce criticism and encourage conformity. We don't explicitly say: 'It is the *similarity* not the difference between people that must govern the message in mass communications.'

A similar answer has to be given to the next defence: that the persuaders are not worse than most of us, only more exposed. It is true, as I have said, that we must take care not to use them as scapegoats instead of looking at more subtle errors. All of us, it is true too, have faults. And we all try in some senses to persuade, particularly in trying to make other people believe the things in which we believe. But that is not necessarily an ill; everything depends on how it is done. All of us introduce extraneous elements into our persuasion; we try some sleight of hand. But most of us try most of the time to be honest; and at some times we come nearer to it than at others. We are free, in that we believe in what we are trying to say; we aren't hired to pretend a passion. We are free to recognize a truth of the subject outside both us (the speakers) and them (our audience). We are free to try to communicate our convictions about the subject as clearly as we can and with all the weight we think it should bear. Then we say, in effect, to our pupils or readers: (I am borrowing from Dr. Leavis, of course) 'This is so, is it not?' That kind of persuasion tries to respect the truth of the subject and the personality of the listener.

The last defence, you may remember, took the form of a counter-charge: that the opponents of advertising are puritan paternalists and much else of a similar kind. This too, like one of its predecessors, is a kind of cheeky *'et tu Brute'*. Still: some opponents *are* the wrong kind of puritan; some are the wrong kind of paternalist; and some are arrogant. And some are indulging in that first refuge of vicariously noble minds —righteous indignation. And some attack the more sharply because they are thwarted or crypto-admen or popular columnists themselves. And some are rascal beadles—they hotly lust to use that whore in that kind for which they whip her.

But again we have no right on these grounds to slide into a bog of indecision crying that we too have faults. We know that we often fail to live up to our own professions and profession; but that does not weaken the case we argue on the basis of that profession. We have to continue, without unnecessary heat, to try to make this case. Not to call for censorship, because censorship is not effective except in certain obvious and not very important ways: but to insist that responsibility of this kind cannot be shrugged off as 'paternalism'; and that 'cultural values' are not 'so-called' after all, but are part of the texture of civilized societies.

Much of the case against the mass persuaders has been implied in the replies to these main lines of defence. I would like now to put it more generally. Look first at the matter of language; and, in the very first place, at the language of advertising apologetics itself. Reading these productions you feel like the narrator in Hemingway's *A Farewell to Arms* when he too heard the big words, the large abstractions:

'I was always embarrassed by the words. There were many words that you could not stand to hear and finally only the names of places had dignity. Abstract words were obscene beside the concrete names of villages. . . .'

Thus it is in the octopoid embrace of the big words of advertising apologetics, whether their ritual grandeurs or their blander intimacies, whether before 'dedicated' or 'sincerity' or 'commitment' or 'creative'.

Or look at the language of the advertisements themselves. Advertising men, when they are talking about their use of language within the advertisements, are particularly fond of that word 'creative'. There is a society which calls itself something like the Creative Advertising Circle. One can well understand. They want to forget that they are hired hacks. A title from that field in which language is used disinterestedly, is used (so to speak) on your own behalf in the search to understand experience, such a title from creative writing acts like a balm. A pawn of the agencies, forced by the increasing separation of functions within a highly industrialized society to put on a verbal enthusiasm for this soap one week and for that petrol the next, how may you survive? You can separate your private life from your professional, probably sealing off the latter behind a coat of protective cynicism; and you can take some pleasure in your own free-wheeling technical skill. But you can't be cynical in public, not if you're an advertiser. And most of us can't be consistently cynical to ourselves about the work which occupies most of our working life and feeds our children. We all need to feel justified. So we call ourselves 'creative copywriters'.

But the copywriter is not a creative writer. That he is intelligent and has a flair for words does not make him a creative writer any more than the possession of a keen colour sense makes a painter. No one can hope to become a creative writer or painter without natural talent. But we only actually become creative artists if we use that talent on certain terms. The terms, at their simplest, are these. A creative writer looks at the object or immerses himself in his experience disinterestedly, and in this very process works through language. His tense relation to language is an integral part of his effort to recreate, understand, order or celebrate that experience. The copywriter looks at the *audience* (that is, the manufacturer's customers) and then at the object—to discover whether anything can be fathered on to the object which will persuade the public to buy it. He applies his verbal skills to finding the images that will make them—the customers over there—buy that over there. This is quite a different process from that of the creative writer; for him the object matters, must matter, more than the audience.

'Tell me what language you use and I'll tell you what kind of man you are,' to alter Ruskin. If you read carefully, you can begin to assess a man's professions by the way he uses words, before you assess the things he actually purports to say. The two may run counter to each other. So—to take a deliberately small example—if a man asserts, so as to make his trade more creditable, that advertising copy will fail unless it has 'the ring of transparent sincerity' we can begin by noting the tired cliché-effect of the expected adjective with the overused noun; and we can point to the typical slip into confusing appearance with reality (not 'the copywriter should be sincere' but '[his copy] should have *the ring of . . .*' i.e. should give the impression of being . . .). From even so slight a sentence we can begin to notice a pattern of attitudes which is being accurately reflected in the language itself.

It is not a small matter if we misuse language. Every time we do so we, even if very slightly, damage our capacity to see straight. We slightly confuse our own experience and risk having a similar effect on some of our readers. We help to muddy the understanding of thought and feeling. This is a fault we all sometimes fall into. When we are tired we cut our emotional corners, comfort ourselves by rearranging experience in a flattering light, blur the truth of fact and evade the pressure of powerful and worrying emotion . . . and we do this through language. But the advertising copywriter is occupationally required to do these things. It is his craft to use language so as to misapply attitudes and misuse emotions. By these excessive or false applications the professional persuader hinders our (and his own) ability to grasp, say, the true meanings of love or sadness. He diminishes the dignity of our own uncertainties and fears. He has presumed to understand, as quite a simple matter, what moves us; and he has *used* this presumed knowledge. Hamlet was one of the first to attack the manipulators, when he turned on Rosencrantz and Guildenstern. They had been so smoothly understanding and sympathetic with Hamlet that they might have freshly taken a course in public relations. Hamlet rounded on them and offered Guildenstern a recorder which Guildenstern confessed to being unable to play:

G. But these I cannot command to any utterance of harmony, I have not the skill.

H. Why look you now, how unworthy a thing you make of me; you would play upon me; you would seem to know my stops; you would pluck out the heart of my mystery; you would sound me from my lowest note, to the top of my compass: . . . why do you think that I am easier to be played on, than a pipe?

Hamlet's anger was keen, not simply because they were the creatures of the king, but for more personal reasons. He was outraged because they had regarded him as a thing of a few obvious drives who could easily be manipulated. I'd like to start a fund to provide framed copies of that passage for every advertising agency office.

The persuaders speak to the dream of perfection and harmony which we all sometimes have. They claim to make the dream real and easily available. But they do so by foreshortening perspectives, by offering a constant succession of immediate rewards, instant perfections and imitation Shangri-La's. The dream of harmony and perfection becomes a weakness and an evasion. Yet it is really one of our more hopeful impulses—when it is enmeshed with a sense also of the difficulty, the delicacy and the slowness of growth towards better understanding. So when the advertisers say that they can 'teach the art of living'; or that they can 'sell more ideas more cheaply than any other'; or that 'there's no limit to the wonderful things advertising can be made to sell . . . religion, social conscience, racial tolerance, education . . .'

L   161

we have to reply that this is the most egregious claim of all, that these things are matters of personal commitment, that no one has the right to intervene in our efforts to find the truth for ourselves, except people who are disinterested.

These claims are also dangerous. If you 'sell' social conscience in the way you sell soap you might soon find yourself selling race-hatred under another government. There is only one word for this process: not persuasion, but propaganda. Through propaganda you 'sell' an idea to people by any available means. Through education you try to help people arrive at convictions for themselves.

I turn now to suggestions about practice, more briefly. I am going to suggest guiding principles rather than specific instances. I see three main lines.

I think we should at the right ages and stages introduce our pupils to the elements of the general debate I have outlined. Probably this is best presented as it arises naturally in the course of other work. On these occasions we can take up with peculiar relevance different parts of the total argument. The students too will be in a better position to assess our opinions than if we had produced a generalized statement. It is easy to blow our tops about the iniquities of the persuaders —and our pupils will probably enjoy it too. But there may not be much to choose between our methods and those of the persuaders then. The rules aren't relaxed because we think we are on the side of the angels.

Also, we should do a lot of practical analysis. For reasons that I have already given, the heart of this will be verbal analysis, the analysis of language. We should also work from the known as much as we can and this will involve the analysis of media which are not primarily verbal but which our pupils know well; for example, T.V., film, pop song. So there are several sub-sections here. One is practice in clear thinking and logical analysis; many years ago I used to do this in adult educational classes, using such books as Thouless and Stebbing. Those books are quite old now, though no doubt still useful. But we probably need some newer aids. The next subsection is concerned with practical criticism (especially comparative criticism) and culture-and-environment analysis; it works, of course, through close study of the language of passages, their nature, assumptions and direction. There is, as most people know, a line of books in this field from Leavis and Thompson onwards, designed for different types and ages of pupil. In the third sub-section—in working from what is already known to our pupils—we are dealing with material which speaks in some ways to their imaginations, about whose forms they are knowledgeable and towards which they are sometimes quite sharply discriminating. It is easy to dismiss all this kind of work as discreditable; equally, it is easy to fail to make the hard distinctions within it that have to be made if the work is to have educational value. But in trying to make these distinctions the pupils' interest and their existing discriminations can be a help. A good deal is being tried out here, in schools of various types as well as in training colleges. But there are still many places where to analyse, say, television programmes would be regarded with unexamined mistrust.

These three kinds of work—clear thinking, practical criticism, the analysis of material well known to our pupils—make up what I am calling the second line of approach. It is delicate work in all sorts of ways. We need to remember that good emotions may be put into bad art; and that there is a danger of driving out sentimentality by putting in smart alec'ery. This kind of work has to be done with exceptional care, with respect for what may sometimes be being brought to, and even taken from, the most meretricious art, with a sense of the tentacular roots on which the enjoyment even of processed art can draw. We have to try to do all this without being soft, or forfeiting standards.

My third line is the most important. To put it as a very obvious statement first: we ought to make the foundations of our work positive. That is to say—the best way of opposing the misuse of language which the mass persuaders encourage is to give our pupils the chance of responding to language

used so as to see experience honestly. That more than anything else will, by contrast, override and put into its place the
manipulative language. If you have read, really read and
felt the weight of, a good novel about human relationships,
then the soap advertisements, the strip cartoons about
nightcaps, the silly situation-comedies all may begin to find
their own places. Our pupils have to be given every possible
chance of responding to good art working in its own way.
This doesn't mean that they have to be outfaced with
'classics' for which they are not ready. But we are beginning
to know much more about the ways the imagination can be
fed at different ages, through the work of some gifted writers
and teachers. We have to be firm here, to say that only the
best is good enough, or we shall be talked into accepting
something that looks 'more reasonable' but evades the real
tests. Our pupils must have a chance, suitable to their years
but not predigested and denatured, to meet the challenge of
complex and honest explorations of experience.

Finally, something about our general temper before this
range of questions about persuasion, freedom and responsibility. I do not think we should feel like last-ditchers. The
persuaders do not lead society by the nose. They are basically
its creatures. Therefore they will always have at least to start
from the educational level, the level of knowledge and self-
awareness, which in spite of them and with some help from
us our pupils have reached. If we manage to lift the level of
discrimination the advertisers will follow like our shadows.

Nor should we be easily optimistic. We shouldn't underestimate the levelling and stiffening effect the mass persuaders *can* have and are having. Some teachers—as I said at
the start—are caught in this process themselves and unconsciously subscribe to the mass persuaders' assumptions. They
therefore feed back into society the sort of people the persuaders seek. They assist that conforming and mirroring
which the persuaders need and encourage; by contrast, increased individuation and self-assumed responsibility *should*
be among their main aims as teachers.

Nor should we flatter ourselves that the whole business is a case of 'Them' and 'Us'. As for 'us', we discriminate; as for 'them', they soak up the ads. As for 'us', we read the *Observer*; as for 'them', they fall for the *Sunday Mirror*. When we feel like that we ought to take an astringent look at the advertisements in the 'serious' Sunday papers, or at the composition of the audiences for the bigger quiz shows or for the glossier women's magazines.

In ways deeper and more complicated than most of us know we are all involved in this process. This fact (as well as my earlier reminder that the advertisers are not principals but agents and victims) ought to tell us, finally, that our suspicion of mass persuasion has to be a double one. We have to be suspicious, as I've spent so much time arguing, of false persuasion in itself, as a hindrance to our right to find our own ways or to be helped only by those who respect us. More important, we should be suspicious of the increasing ramifications of mass persuasion because what we are being persuaded towards is not only or more importantly to buy this soap or that holiday or that style of clothing. We are being persuaded to buy this way of looking at life, of having opinions about life, of expecting this rather than that from life, from other people and from ourselves. We are being asked to accept unquestioned the assumptions of that sort of society in which mass commercial persuasions themselves best flourish.

We are back, then, with the whole problem of changing values in a changing society, a society which finds it more than usually hard to understand itself, but is tempted to think that the movement and direction inherent in increasingly complex societies and conducive to their smoother running . . . that this is self-justifying. We can't afford to ignore this issue or to reduce its scale. We should push as well as we can through our own work for more scepticism and imaginative honesty. At our backs, supporting us as teachers, we have always the experience of great art—and the chance of learning from its integrity.

8

STEPHEN POTTER

Learning to enjoy

Learning to enjoy. I am delighted to have been set this fine theme, although it is tougher than I first thought. It seemed to me that there were three or four ways of tackling it, and at first I had no luck. They didn't come to anything. Obviously I might collect 'the best of what has been thought and said' on the subject, and base my remarks on that. I happen to have half-a-dozen Dictionaries of Quotations. I rather fancy myself at using quotations as if they had come to me spontaneously out of a full mind. But I didn't find one quotable line. Not one.

Then I thought I might struggle with *definitions* of joy and learning, and almost immediately I found myself turning into the old forgotten type of lawyer's clerk or civil servant—the type who (this was in New Zealand quite recently) examined a proposed site for a new playground. He wrote in his report:

'It is obvious from the difference in elevation with relation to the short depths of the property that the contour is such as to preclude any reasonable development potential for active recreation.'

He meant that the site was too sloping, I think.

The most satisfying method of course would be to give you the distilled experience evolved by a wise yet self-questioning man from a lifetime of bold and arduous experiment in the pursuit of true selfhood. If I admit, as I must, that I am not the man for this, I must now seriously ask you to appreciate the fact that it is not from egotism that I have had to choose a simpler method altogether.

I want to give you my own experience. My experience as a twentieth century-er. My own attempts, and failures, in learning to enjoy. Early mistakes. Later a few half-successes.

Under 'Joy' in my stock of trite quotations comes 'Youth's the Season made for Joys'. Is that true? How did it work for me? (Let me say at once that so far as falling in love is concerned, it becomes progressively *more* pleasurable or at any rate *less agonizing* up to 50.) But I mean much earlier—childhood pleasures. In retrospect they seem immeasurably more intense than anything one has experienced since. *But were they?*

It is difficult for us to remember our enjoyment of the pure and virginal *senses*. Not the sense of sight, of course, because the eye of a child is so often turned inward, to the world of fancy: but the senses of touch and smell and taste. Charles Dickens is wonderful here—describing for instance the intensity of David Copperfield's life by nose, as it were. The fishy smell of the delightful houseboat at Yarmouth, the smell of stables at the coach-station in London, the Salem House smells in schoolroom and dining-room, the foggy atmosphere of the morning when the news of his mother's death came, the 'breathless smell of warm black crepe' in the undertaker's shop.

The nose of the child is like the eye of the poet. Then I think of myself, age 10, looking forward after cricket practice to a taste of the ice-cream cornet at the little shop across the road. In 1910 they cost a halfpenny. The exquisite pleasure— but then, of course I had five times the number of taste buds, buds for sweetness on the front half of the tongue. It must have seemed as good as, now perhaps, the most perfect Zabaglioni ever produced by Boulestin's. When the mind is as sensitive to sight as unexposed films, merely to go to London by electric tram seems fantastic luck . . . it was just as I hoped . . . by making a rush for it I could get the seat just behind the driver, and stare at the fine red neck of this great man, and his blue coat blown out stiff as a bell by the wind.

Or what else, a little later? Glorious Gilbert and Sullivan at the Kennington Theatre, my cheeks burning with excitement before I got there, and never a mouldy thought that Sullivan was already a bit old fashioned, and intellectually, too tuneful altogether, and (some idiot said) basically inferior to Offenbach. Or reading the first really big novel. The grown-ups' novel. Looking forward to getting to bed so that I could read, all alone, *Vanity Fair*. 'And George lay dead on the battlefield.' Never to be forgotten, the look at that moment of my shadowy room, or the refuse of wax round the candle. It seemed to me that, through my tears, I saw life, at last and finally. This was tragedy. I was happy.

Intense pleasures—but are they perfect? Are they the best? Not so, surely. Youth's joys are hampered by various drawbacks. For one thing these early pleasures are seldom, except for the infant, absolutely pure. My third halfpenny ice-cream cornet may have been slightly soured by my mother's, 'Not too many ice-creams, darling,' or, 'Don't spoil your appetite.' There is often, in other words, a slight sense of guilt. Reading *Vanity Fair*, I still had to worry. Would anybody see the light through the door, even if I stuffed my dressing-gown against it? A little later I was at my main school, a day school, Westminster, which meant that I did my prep. at home. Livy, Book II . . . 15 lines of the Aeneid to learn by heart, Exercise 15, Rutherford's Greek Grammar. But first, let me slide into the piano room. I was learning to fumble out the slow movement of Beethoven's piano sonata op. 10, No. 3, those chords seemed to send extraordinary vibrations all up my arm. 'Have you done your work, Stephen?' They weren't discouraging me from music, far from it—but what would my form master, Holy Herbert, say in Latin, next morning? I had a guilty feeling mixed with this superb pleasure. In fact it wasn't for ten years, when I saw that Bernard Shaw had written, 'My chief education was the Beethoven piano sonatas,' that the load of guilt was finally lifted, and lifted from many such pleasures. The non-conformist conscience is buried deep in the twentieth century, but professors of enjoyment must pull it out by the root.

Another notable difference of these early pleasures is the familiar fact that most of them—Gilbert and Sullivan, the halfpenny cornet—are even better before they happen. Christmas Day is a little spoilt by the thought of the anti-climax of after-Christmas. The August holiday in the Isle of Wight has been going on inside the boy's head for two months before it began. Already by August 2nd the tiny black seed, not yet moving but present, has been planted. August 28th is only four weeks off.

'Don't speak to me,' I used to shout inside myself, coming out of the theatre, after seeing the play about the Flag Lieutenant, whose face was covered with the blood of the Bashi-Bazouk. 'Did you enjoy it, darling?' Of course—but why say it? Anyhow no more theatre for a month: and a month is the same as for ever.

Indeed most of these intense childhood pleasures are tainted by the thought that next day the treat will be over, and back will come the boredoms which are greater in childhood than at any other time of life, if only because they seem to last a hundred years. The greatest boredom of all, of course, is school next morning. Can any child learn how to enjoy this time? I doubt it: the best I could do was to try and forget it, by creating a kind of convulsive agony in which I prevented myself from brooding on the agony by doing everything at the last moment. This I did particularly with the journey to Westminster School from home. Our home was a mile from Wandsworth Common Station which was at best 11 minutes from Victoria: yet I solemnly assure you that I was able to get up at 8 minutes to nine, wash and do teeth (30 secs.), dress, have breakfast and get to my seat in Poet's Corner at 9.30 exactly.

Cancelling out one agony by another is scarcely the right way of learning how to enjoy. It is the opposite of the right way. But first of all I had to realize the enjoyment of learning.

It so happened that for me it was never through a school-master. Somebody outside school—whom I admired. Who had authority. There were my cousins at Warlingham, a little bit older than me and therefore heroes. They had a loft full of shavings and the smell of oil, and a whetstone, and a phono-graph, a real phonograph, built to take the old cylindrical record. There was only one record, and while we mucked about with screwdrivers and saws it was on, all the time. My cousins, mechanically minded, were right to think this a mechanical marvel. After the hundredth hearing I could agree—but to me the marvel was the music, the name meant nothing—'Elgar's Wand of Youth Suite'—the march, which starts ungainly and then suddenly shifts into a change of key, delicately *vivace*, mysterious. It opened the door, for me, to a new kind of music. I can never hear it without excitement, and without smelling the shavings. And it was all due, originally, to the authority of my cousins—at least three years older than me.

Kind authority. Let kind authority influence you. That was how history first came alive to me, I think. Facts about The Five Mile Act and the Council of Trent stuck in my in-tellectual gullet for years. You remember 1066?

Arrange in this order
(1) Henry I
(2) Henry II
(3) Henry III

Do not write on both sides of the paper at once.

Undigestible facts were dislodged by an uncle of mine just because he had the power to say, 'Look.' Suddenly he would get off his bicycle. 'Cultivation terraces,' he would say en-thusiastically, pointing to shadows on the hills near Worth Matravers, 'Most interesting.' Then prehistoric man really existed! (It was H. G. Wells who said of Rebecca West that the great thing about her was that she had the power to say, 'Look.') 'Scratch dial,' my uncle would say, his thick spec-tacles almost touching a small hole on the east jamb of an old church door. I began to see scratch dials everywhere. Once they had shown the times of mass. 'Pre-Reformation' meant something.

I was late in appreciating poetry, but admired authority came to my help again. *Be influenced*—I had not yet formulated that rule, but I was acting on it, if the authority was really to my taste. That new short story by my hero, Rudyard Kipling—I read them all as they first came out. It was called 'Wireless'. A young chemist, fiddling with his home-made crystal set, was getting something, through the ether. Words across space—and across time, too? 'Beaded bubbles . . . sunburnt mirth . . . amid the alien corn.' Words from the past, from Keats. And the fact that Kipling was framing these words so reverently in this not very successful story made me reverence them too. It was the beginning of poetry, for me—and of course as I got on to Keats and Shakespeare, I discarded Kipling scornfully. Discarding scornfully is *not* the way to learn to enjoy. Later, when I got back to Kipling, I realized that it was the rhythms of his little verses in the Jungle Book, sticking in my head, which had made the transition to the appreciation of other people's poetry so easy.

Now let me pause a moment, for a natural break. I have gone quite a way without talking of *learning* to enjoy. Perhaps it is about this time I have reached in this story, the age of twenty, that we begin to have an inkling that such things are possible. I am sticking to personal examples—you will probably be able to think of much better ones from your own life. All these children now seem to go abroad for their holidays, almost automatically. Not so in days of yore. It was partly because of the first war. By the age of 20 I had scarcely been outside England and I had an intolerable itch to see new countries. 'Education,' I said to myself, but in fact my motive was scalp hunting. Cross them off the list.

I took my bicycle to Paris and started off towards the Moselle. 'See the war sites.' See them? Not a bit of it. Crossing them off. Cross off Luxembourg—and by turning left at Cologne, cross off Germany, Holland and Belgium as well in one scalp hunting fortnight. A later universities journey to

Vienna, Budapest and Warsaw—how historically marvellous that should have been. I can still see a tall superb red-headed Jew striding through the Warsaw Ghetto. . . . But it meant almost nothing—because I was travelling on an intellectually empty stomach. I came without knowledge—'with an open mind', in other words, which really meant a closed one.

Next time, my sister took me to Florence, I was not going to let her be one up on me in knowing all about it: so almost by chance I read it up. Spent mornings in the National Gallery. Read about Neri and Bianchi, Guelphs and Ghibellines. The result of course was that Florence really meant something, was never forgotten. Complete transformation. It was my first real step in learning to enjoy. Work, in order to enjoy.

Soon we realize that it is possible to apply this principle of preparation—'boning up' the Americans call it—to almost anything. Enjoy more, by learning first. Take music. I was 'tremendously musical'—but was I? Age 20, and particularly keen, at the moment on Handel. But knowing nothing really later than Mendelssohn? I didn't even know the Beethoven quartets. Remember that this was pre-radio, pre-L.P. and, for me pre-Proms, though I was just *about* to gorge myself on them. Perhaps, if I learned. . . .

For instance. What did 'the cacophany of Stravinsky' mean, in the *Westminster Gazette*? Stravinsky music certainly bored me too, at a concert. Yet the ballet people thought he was marvellous. Suppose I worked a little. And sure enough, sitting in front of a gramophone playing the first record of Petroushka every day for a fortnight, it did get in—it did penetrate—and the doorway was swung wide open therefore of course for Wagner and Elgar as well, besides Vaughan Williams and the 'modern' music which succeeded them. Besides the rest of Stravinsky. (Verdi almost incredibly, was not really intellectually U in those days . . . Verdi and Wagner have now swapped places, in reputation. If I had to name one villain of the piece, one spoil-sport, in learning to enjoy, my choice would be Intellectual Fashion.)

'Learn to enjoy'—you will note that the word is 'learn', not 'teach'. 'Learn,' not 'be taught.' Outside assistance, un-asked, never seems to work so well—may even be a handicap which needs overcoming. Take the enjoyment of Shake-speare. Here the teachers are only too ready to weigh in with their advice. The editors, the theorists, the introducers. A university student, who has chosen the superb subject of English Literature, when he turns to Shakespeare may feel the whole weight of it all to be too much. Here, to enjoy, he must ruthlessly discard. Young students can usually do this with their most powerful weapon—satire, or parody. You remember those footnotes. Well, in those days, in the Edition Recommended, the footnotes did not *need* parody, only quotation. I used to collect them.

(*Midsummer Night's Dream*)
> And I serve the fairy queen,
> To dew her orbs upon the green:

orbs: generally called 'fairy rings' and supposed to be created by the growth of a species of fungus, *Agaricus Orcades*, Linn. These circles are usually from four to eight feet broad, and from six to twelve feet in diameter, and are more prominently marked in summer than in winter. . . . But see Mr. Sidney Turner (*British Medical Journal*, 28th July 1894), who considered the 'so-called "fairy rings"' were produced by the fungi, which composed the ring of the previous year. . . .'

(*Henry IV, p.* 2)
> (*L. Bard.* Who keeps the gate here, ho!)

Who . . . here, ho! 'Who' is here, I think, the indefinite (i.e. 'He who') and not the interrogative pronoun, as is implied, for instance, by the punctuation, 'Who keeps the gate here? Ho!' (*Oxford Shakespeare*) and 'Who keeps the gate here, ho?' (*Cambridge Shakespeare*). 'Who keeps the gate' is a periphrasis (i.e. 'Porter') of a kind usual in calling to servants or other, in attendance but out of sight. Cf. 2 Henry VI, l, iv, 82: '*York* . . . Who's within there, ho! Enter a *Serving Man*' (*Oxford Shakespeare*); Henry VIII, V, ii, 2, 3: 'Cran . . . Ho! Who waits there!' ('there?' *Oxford Shakespeare*) Enter Keeper';

(*Antony and Cleopatra*)
> 'This foul Egyptian has betrayed me . . . Triple-turn'd whore'

triple turn'd. This refers, of course, to the three infidelities of Cleopatra: (*a*) to Julius Caesar for Pompey, (*b*) to Pompey for Antony, (*c*) to Antony for Octavius.

Once I had collected these, and enjoyed them with my friends, they ceased to bother me. We settled down to enjoy Shakespeare.

Learning to enjoy. This sometimes takes the form of learning a subject as an alternative to being bored by it. Let me explain. Very often the feeling that a subject is boring beyond hope can, if it is intense enough, be the prelude to a first curiosity, or interest. So it happened to me. I used to love long walking—(hiking, but to beg a hitch in those days was difficult, unusual, and would be considered unsporting). So an April walk from Warwick to St. Ives meant really walking. If you average twenty-three miles a day, good health turns to super health, and the brain goes to sleep. But it was meant to be a literary walk for me—I wanted for instance to cross the Quantocks by Nether Stowey. There was Coleridge's cottage, safe and sound. And there, blow me down, was a 'last red leaf' left over from last year. No doubt it was beech leaf, the colour of tobacco-stained fingers, you know? But I didn't know. Because the fact is that although Coleridge and Wordsworth and therefore, surely, I, were 'nature lovers', the subject of trees and wild-flowers had always filled me with the blackest kind of boredom. I did not know the difference between beech and elm. Dreadful subject. 'Pansies, lilies, kingcups, daisies, Let them live upon their praises.' Secretly, I hated those lines. But . . . what *was* that leaf? Suddenly this thing began to irritate me. It was getting ridiculous. And what was that diseased looking flower at the edge of the stream by Coleridge's house? By chance, the little post office was a little book shop—there was something called the *Wayside Wanderer* series—ghastly title, I thought. But in one little book I found that that leaf was beech, in the other, that the flower was butterbur. Easy. Rather interesting really. Identifying made me look at them hard. The first time I had done such a thing in my life. And my life was completely altered. Walks, golf courses, rubbish heaps, lonely moors, bomb sites later, had for me, a marvellous new dimension added to them. A hundred different kinds of green alone entered into my life. A hundred textures and smells of the crushed leaf. Good old Coleridge—it was not the last time he was to alter my life.

I was 26—and I mention this to remind you of the great enjoyment of learning a new subject a little bit past the normal age. It is not only the subject itself but the fact that you are given new terms of reference. One of the greatest enjoyments of learning is the driving home of a piece of knowledge by the discovery of a cross-reference. The more disrelated the two subjects the better. History was as flat as cardboard to me till I read *Puck of Pook's Hill*—until the fact was made three dimensional by the cross-reference. For my uncle had shown me one of those yon dimpled tracks in a field of wheat near West Hoathly. Plants can often give you that kind of cross-reference. You may as a child find spooky-looking poisonous henbane growing near an old castle, and it may, rightly or wrongly, bring home the fact that some barons really were wicked. I owe two of my biggest 3D fact pleasures to two most undistinguished looking plants. The first was a screwed-up little yellow Cruciferae—a humble member of the mustard family—which was shown to me growing alongside the wheel tracks of a bus route by a bomb site near the Tower of London. It was secretly revealed to me by Louseley, the eminent botanist. It was London Rocket, which had spread across the ruins of the Great Fire in 1666, and hadn't been seen in London for a hundred years. Somehow, the new Fire of wartime London had brought it to life again.

The second was a humble root leaf, a thistle leaf, the 'milk thistle', still found occasionally in England, very common in that great kingdom of majestic thistles, the south coast of Spain. Why was it called Carduus Marianum? Because the beautiful milky veins of the leaf were thought to suggest the milk of the Virgin Mother. Pretty story to be tucked away for twenty years. Then one day I was in Palestine, taking an

exercise walk on the hills round Nazareth. Plenty of thistle
there, and only one kind, or only one I noticed, and I noticed
it very hard indeed. Carduus Marianum.

So far I've been talking mostly about youth enjoyments.
How about when we are older? When *are* we older? When
the gramophone needle sticks in the groove I suggest, and
goes on repeating itself. This may happen, easily, at the age of
only eighteen. I was aware of this and made attempts to
avoid it. It was when I was eighteen, if you will believe me,
that I first became emancipated from Victorianism—that I
first realized Wells, and Shaw came to knock at my door,
'like a brisk neat maid with morning tea', and open the curtains. Bliss to be alive in this great emancipation, I thought,
and in a few years I was in danger of being stuck permanently in *this* groove—of emancipation—long after the
chains were broken. I looked for more. Who could take us
beyond common sense and the scientific attitude? Who believed that we were '*not* contained between our hat and our
boots', as Whitman said? Well, Whitman to start with: Keats
—and I must stick up for Middleton Murry here, and his
great interpretation of Keats. Then there was always Blake.
And Coleridge. This is too big a subject for us at this moment
—let's leave it and call it 'learning to enjoy by learning to
continue to grow'. This would be too big a claim: but there
is no harm in trying.

A second mention of Coleridge reminds me of another way
of learning to enjoy. It could be called, 'Learning to enjoy by
learning.' Here is an experience many of you will share.
When I'd taken my degree in English Literature I thought,
'Well that's done.' 'I've tucked literature under my belt.' So
I thought. Till I began to *teach* Chaucer (at this University!)
Chaucer? Certainly. But to teach him I found I had to take
the subject apart and learn all over again. Then I began to
enjoy it as if for the first time. In other words I had to teach
in order to learn to enjoy. And Coleridge? Of course I knew
him. Did a special paper on the Romantic Revival poets. But
when I was asked to make an edition of him for Nonesuch,

and had to read Coleridge from start to finish, and *incorporate* him within the limitations of my knowledge and experience —then I was truly beginning to know something of a great writer, and that was an enjoyment which I've never lost.

As one gets more fixed in age, these re-orientations become more and more difficult. How is it possible to continue to learn to enjoy? No doubt by learning to be outward looking, rather than inward. Many people do this by pouring themselves into social works. Others by learning to look outward, at the outside world, observing it, appreciating it. Straightforwardly, perhaps, by trying to draw it, paint it. Or by painting it in words, describing. Think of James Boswell, so full of angst, so worried about his reputation, so determined, in spite of his fussy absurdities, to appear manly and dependable, so constantly being disappointed in his attempts to reform his own character. Why was he essentially a happy man? Because he had learned to look at the whole world, including himself, with detachment. How boring, for other people, would be the dinner party at the Duke of Argyll's, on that Highland Journey. Dr. Johnson was pretty silent; the host, peremptory. But Boswell, a little tight, was still watching, noting. Listen.

'A gentleman in company after dinner was desired by the Duke to go to another room for a specimen of curious marble . . . he could not refuse; but to avoid any appearance of servility, he whistled as he walked out of the room, to show his independency.'

What a perfect little water-colour. The enjoyment of observation.

When age comes, there is a danger of losing the enjoyment of learning for ever. Noble angst turns to petty worry. How is my stock? How does Thumpington still manage to get away with it? How can I be like Blake or Goethe or Browning or Picasso who seem to remain happily effective to the end of their lives? One's own idiosyncratic character, which one gets so sick of, is still clanking along, like a tin tied on the tail. When older age comes, in great thick slices, there is a temptation to fall back on enjoying things in retrospect. In a sort of parallel antithesis, the child enjoys in anticipation. There is a tendency not to enjoy *at the moment*, and therefore not to enjoy completely. Hence perhaps the mysterious link between children and the old.

Well, are there any more tips for your approach to Act V, to round all this off? I would say: don't let love of comfort stop you from doing interesting things. One wouldn't quite, now, bicycle seventy miles there and back on the chance of seeing Thomas Hardy rolling his lawn, but one can still make a suitably equivalent attempt. In theatre-going, don't lapse into a liking for happy domestic comedies—'there's quite enough cheerfulness in life without having to go to the theatre for it' (Henry Reed). Study, harder than ever—though not necessarily at the university in Bournemouth, mentioned in last night's Panorama, which advertised daytime lectures on How to Retire. At all times of life learn to continue to enjoy companions by keeping your friendships, to repeat Dr. Johnson's famous advice, 'in a state of constant repair'. To widen your enjoyment of your fellow-men, never pre-judge a man, or go by hearsay. We are for ever indignant with the fearful fits of national indignation which caused the dismissal of Byron and of Oscar Wilde. But we are constantly making exactly such judgements ourselves, quite often on grounds of sexual behaviour, or alcoholic behaviour, or financial behaviour, or a disagreement over loyalties.

I seem, for a moment, to have got on rather a high horse, and I have always been ill at ease on horseback. I have left out such a lot of joys which can be learned. I have left out sex—let's leave the last word on that, for a moment, to Noel Coward, who says that, 'Sex is a form of lighting.' The consolations of religion should indeed be here, only the words 'consolation' and 'religion' seem to me deeply incompatible.

Let me lower the tone, and lift it at the same time, by ending with a word on that most necessary joy that men must learn—the ability to be psychologically, even if we can't hope to be physically, presentable enough to recommend themselves, in companionship, to a woman. Let Virginia Woolf say why:

'Women have served all these centuries as looking-glasses possessing the magic and delicious power of reflecting the figure of man at twice its natural size. Without that power probably the earth would still be swamp and jungle. . . . How is he to go on giving judgment, civilising natives, making laws, writing books, dressing up and speechifying at banquets, unless he can see himself at least twice the size he really is?'

Woman is an enjoyment which men must most humbly and ardently learn.

9

SIR HUGH FOOT

Learning to live in a heterogeneous world

I wish to speak to you on the importance of relationships between peoples of different races and nationalities, and on the evils and the dangers of race hatred and violence and, most important of all, on the measures which we can and should take to bring about better international understanding. These are the subjects I care most about in the world and I shall speak to you about them from my own experience and my own conviction.

When I was twenty-one years of age I left my own University of Cambridge and went to Jerusalem. It was my first appointment—and every one of us, I am sure, remembers very clearly the detailed circumstances of his first arrival in his first post. I very well remember arriving at the railway station at Jerusalem. I imagined that my arrival in the Near East was an event of some world consequence, and I was depressed to find that there was no one there to meet me: I stood disconsolate on the railway station in Jerusalem on that bright Sunday morning.

I soon discovered why there was no one there to meet me. It was a time of tension, of anticipated violence. It was expected that at any moment tension between the Arabs and the Jews would lead to an explosion. The dispute was about the Wailing Wall where the Jews wept for the loss of King Solomon's temple and the Moslems claimed the same area as part of the holy Haram Ash Shareef. At any moment, I was told, the intense feeling between the two communities in Palestine was likely to lead to violence. Within a day or two of my arrival the explosion came. I heard first the ugly sound in the distance of the mob coming from the Mosque of Omar and pressing through the narrow streets of the old city. Then I saw the crowd come out through the Damascus Gate waving guns and sticks and chanting with a rhythmic fury that I came to know well in later years of riot and rebellion. Later on I saw where the mob had gone from one end of the long street to the other killing man, woman and child as it went. That was my first experience in my first post. Still, more than thirty years later, the Holy City is divided by the scar of barbed wire running through the centre of the city with men watching day and night in constant enmity. I learnt in that first week and in subsequent years of disorder and rebellion the principal lesson of my life—that evil that is done when men are divided by fear and hatred and violence.

I thank God that in other parts of the world and in later years I have been able to learn how much good can be done when men are united in constructive endeavour.

My last overseas post before I went to the United Nations at New York was in Cyprus which is, as we know, a meeting place between East and West, between Christendom and Islam. When I went there as Governor the two communities —each backed from outside the island—seemed to be condemned to increasing violence and disorder. But nevertheless it was possible, eventually, to shake hands with Archbishop Makarios, the leader of the Greek community in the island, and at the same time with Dr. Kutchuk, the leader of the Turkish community, and sail away from an island—not with its problems solved, or its animosities removed; certainly not, but with the killing temporarily stopped and with both Greeks and Turks having agreed to work to establish a Republic together.

Before that I was concerned with an even greater world problem. I was for seven years Governor of Jamaica. There were many problems in Jamaica but our principal purpose was to show that people of different racial origin could work together in equality. It was possible to prove in Jamaica that democracy need know no frontiers of race or colour. There have been failures in the West Indies: there was the failure of the West Indian Federation which many of us hoped would bring together the three million people of the British territories of the West Indies. But far more important than that was the contribution which Jamaica and other islands in the West Indies have been able to make in establishing a full democratic system in communities made up of different races.

Before that I worked with the peoples of Nigeria, the state with by far the greatest population in Africa. We were working with all the different people of Nigeria to establish a free federation. I often used to think that there were more differences amongst the people of Nigeria than there are, for instance, amongst the peoples of Europe—far more differences between a Nigerian Northerner and an Ibo and a Yoruba than there are between an Englishman and a Greek or a Spaniard. Our task was to work with the people themselves, to bring together all these different peoples with their different languages and religions and origin and outlook and character into one single nation represented in one single parliament. Those of us who served in Nigeria will not forget the night when the green and white flag of the Independent Federation of Nigeria was raised and the Prime Minister turned to us and said, 'We thank the British officers who have worked with us through the years, who came to us first as masters, then as leaders, and now as partners; but always as friends.' If there is to be an obituary for the Colonial Service we would not want a better obituary than that.

What was the training of our service? It was very simple and very rough and ready, but very effective. In all the territories which we administered—in India, in the old days; in the Far East; in East, West, Central Africa; in Palestine where I was—the system was much the same. Take a young man, say twenty-five years of age, who has been only a year or two in the territory to which he is posted. Make him a District Officer. He may have a few doctors, engineers, teachers to help him, but this young man is fully responsible for the whole range of government activity within his District. Leave him there for five or six years—to get to know the language; to work with the people, to share their hopes, their aspirations, their disappointments, their setbacks. At the end of that period—there is no merit or credit in this, the effect is automatic—that young man becomes wholly devoted to the interests of the people of his District. He fights higher authority to get for the people of his District what he thinks they need and deserve. It is good training for a Governor. When I was Governor of Jamaica I did not look on myself as the agent of Whitehall; I regarded myself as the advocate of Jamaica. And when I was asked to go back to Cyprus when many people told me that no conceivable solution was in sight, I was glad to go back because I knew and loved the people of Cyprus. I thought that if we put their interests first we might be able to find the key to a problem which had defied all efforts at solution.

And so in the service to which I belonged we proudly claim that we have come most of the way. Now of the six hundred and sixty-six million people in the British Commonwealth all except 3 per cent are in countries self-governing and independent. I used to enjoy telling the Soviet representatives at the United Nations that we in the British Commonwealth have enfranchised and brought into the councils of the world in sixteen or seventeen years nearly three times the total population of the whole Soviet Union. I also used to remind my American colleagues that of all the countries previously under British administration which have achieved independence all have by the free vote of their people decided to remain within the British Commonwealth—all, that is, except four. The four you know: Burma, Ireland, South Africa and the United States of America. We were in a better position than most to know the mistakes. It is not for us to attempt to belittle the evils which arose and which still arise from colonialism. But we were proud of what we did. That is not in any way inconsistent with being concerned about the present, and gravely alarmed about the future.

Complacency is the greatest danger. We like to push the troubles of the world away from us and to carry on with our own self-centred interests. It is not for me to attempt any catalogue of world dangers. We look round the world and we see dangers—great dangers—everywhere. Dangers arising from poverty: a thousand million people in the world are living just above, or at, or even below, the starvation level. And the population of the world at the present rate of increase will double in less than fifty years. The likelihood is that the two-thirds of the world which are poor will drag down in chaos the third of the world which is now affluent.

We do not have to look far for more immediate dangers. We think of the dangers of the false frontiers which are the evil legacy of colonialism. Soon there may well be armed hostility between two African States—between Somalia and Kenya. We see the tension which exists between the new Malaysia and the huge, scattered territory of Indonesia. It is well for us to remember that these frontier dangers arise not from the present decisions of the Africans or the Asians but from the past actions of Europeans. If there were fighting between Somalia and Kenya they would not be fighting about any frontier made by the Somalis or by the Kenyans— they would be fighting about frontiers which arose from the colonial penetrations of Great Britain and Italy into Somalia in years gone by; they would be fighting about frontiers which were laid down by ourselves and our allies when we were in full control at the end of the last war. Who made the frontiers between Malaysia and Indonesia? Not the Malaysians; not the Indonesians. They were made in the days of colonial expansion and domination by the British and the Dutch in the Far East. So there is no cause for complacency or superiority on our part. Colonialism is almost dead but the legacy of colonialism in the false frontiers established by

European greed and European expansion will remain to curse the new countries for generations to come.

Another danger which we see day by day in Africa is the danger of tribalism, a danger which may yet cause the whole of the Congo to disintegrate. That was the danger—I pray that it may have passed—in Kenya. It was the danger at one time in the Gold Coast, as it was then called. Certainly it was the danger in Nigeria. These dangers are not wholly removed. But let us also remember that in this too we carry a heavy responsibility. Until very recently we, through our processes and policies of indirect rule, were encouraging separatist tribalism. Too long we refused to accept or to encourage the creation of wider national movements. There are dangers whichever way we look but all of them, it seems to me, are insignificant compared with the main danger which we face today, the danger of a race war which will involve the whole world.

African nationalism has advanced through West Africa, through East Africa, into Central Africa, right down to the River Zambesi. North of the river you have the Africans in full charge of their destinies—in all the countries north of the River Zambesi. But south of the river no African has any say in the policy of the government of his country. This force of nationalism—one of the greatest forces of our generation, of our century—comes right down, as I say, to the River Zambesi. South of the river you have the principle of white domination maintained—with powerful forces to maintain it. Who can imagine that that confrontation between African nationalism and white domination which we see in Africa now—who can imagine that it will be resolved without a long and bitter and bloody convulsion?

I sometimes try, when I have been speaking in the United States, to give some picture of how Africa appears to me in these days. It looks to me like a great house in which in each room the work goes forward separately. Few of us would pass an examination on the names of all the new states of Africa: the names of these the separate rooms in the house. You look into one room and you see the work encouraging, courageous, admirable. You look into another room and you are doubtful, anxious about what's being done there. You look into another separate room and you feel that things are going dreadfully wrong. But the work goes forward—the effort goes forward—in each of the separate rooms. While down in the cellars already the fuses are lit which threaten explosions—to blow not only the cellars but the whole house sky high. When blood flows then there will be no more moderate leaders in Africa. It is difficult, I admit, to bring one's imagination to picture what will happen. It will not be an open battle between armies in a field: it will of course be subversive warfare. I have had some experience of it in Palestine and in Cyprus. In Cyprus we had thirty thousand troops and never more than a hundred rebels against us at any given time. You have to picture the situation in South Africa where the fighting will not be fighting openly by one army against another but by the methods of subversive warfare—the methods of the Mau Mau. And then on the other side you have to picture what the reactions to that will be. Domination will be maintained by the fiercest methods. You have to picture what a South African O.A.S. will be like. And when you put those—not possibilities—approaching certainties together you have to consider what effect that will have on every country in the world and indeed on every individual.

I have spoken of complacency. Now let me say a word about superiority. In our dealings with these, the new peoples of Asia and Africa, we use the words—'emotional', 'reckless', 'utterly lacking in responsibility'. But surely we should have the imagination to be able to put ourselves in the position of the new African, for instance—the new educated African who is told that all he must do is to imitate civilized, Christian Europe. He looks at the modern history of Europe. And you cannot blame him if he is somewhat perplexed. He knows that twice within a lifetime we in Europe have been engaged in bloody massive conflicts that make his tribal wars look like child's play. He sees tyranny; he sees furious disputes. Who should he imitate? Should he imitate Salazar of Portugal or Franco of Spain? or, going back, should he imitate Hitler or Chamberlain? Albania or Yugoslavia? East or West? where is he to look to get his perfect example of Christian civilization? The Africans have in the past had to accept the leadership and the domination of white people not only in government but also in the churches and in commerce and in every walk of life. Only within living memory have they first questioned and then rejected the infallibility of the European. Mr. Sithole, one of the leaders of Southern Rhodesia, tried to explain the Africans' disillusion by quoting Caliban: 'What a thrice double ass was I to treat this drunkard as a god and worship this dull fool.' Who can blame the Africans if they come to the conclusion that it is we who have been misguided? Who can blame them if they decide to think for themselves and come to their own conclusions?

I have said something about complacency and superiority. Now let me speak about our arrogance in our approach to the people of Asia and Africa. It seems to me that the danger of racialism comes not from those who oppose racial domination but from those who attempt to maintain it by force— and from those who condone it. My oldest friend in Africa, now the Nigerian Ambassador to the United Nations, Chief Adebo, told me the other day that the things he learnt from England he hears in these days from Africans but very seldom from Englishmen. We have no indignation, apparently, when we see injustice or exploitation or mass cruelty. We show no determination to assist in the ending of political slavery.

We must think of these questions of race relations, of course, not only in political terms but also in human terms. Several years ago when I was in Jamaica I knew a Jamaican who was—to use these horrible terms—a slightly coloured Jamaican of good family who had married a white American. They lived in Jamaica amongst friends of all races and communities and they brought up their children without having

187

to make them realize the miseries and the injustices of racial discrimination. The daughter of ten years old became sick and the father set out with her urgently for medical advice to New York. They went to Miami by plane, and then on by the train. They were travelling in the train through Florida to New York when, having gone so far, they were removed because they were coloured from the train, which specially stopped at a wayside station. My friend and his daughter had to wait for a train which carried coloured people. Stop to think of what must have gone on in the mind of that girl on that station that night. Stop to think, too, that hundreds of thousands of children in the world, brought up in the love and care of their families, have suddenly to understand—to have it explained to them—that the love they know in their own families is something which stops at their front doors, that there are many people in the world who will treat them as inferiors solely because of their colour. What a terrible thing for a child to discover.

If I am right in thinking that the greatest danger in the world is the danger of a race war starting in Africa, who will deal with it? Will the Americans go in? Not very willingly. Will the Russians go in? Will the Chinese uphold their claim to be the new champions of the coloured people of the world? Conceivably. I think it is true that if one great nation goes in the others go in too. Such is the danger of world conflict.

In facing that danger let me now turn to speak about new men and new ideas and new motives and the role of the new nations.

I like to speak about the new nations because all my life I have lived and worked with Arabs and Africans and West Indians. These new nations, which now constitute a majority in the United Nations, with all their differences and with all their difficulties have certain similarities. They have certain characteristics in common.

The first characteristic which is common to the new nations of Asia and Africa is they are good judges of us. When you are a subject people you have to be expert in your so-called masters. When you are a colonial people under the domination of a foreign power you have to make a close study of those who are in authority over you. I sometimes say that I in my life have had to write hundreds, maybe thousands, of confidential reports on government officials; but I always knew I could write a far better report on my superior than I could about my subordinate. It is not necessary to tell the leaders of Africa and Asia about the United States of America or about this country—most of them have been educated here or there. You needn't tell the President of Nigeria or the President of Ghana about the United States of America: they were educated there. And many of the leaders, as we know, have been educated in this country. I sometimes think they know us too well. At any rate they are not going to be fooled by the British or by the Russians or by the Americans or by the French. I suggest to you that that is one good thing.

And the next characteristic which is common to them all is that they are determined to think for themselves. You may think that that is obvious enough, but until quite recently the official attitude in the United States of America, as well as in this country, was that all that was expected of these new nations when they became independent was that they should step up smartly, say which side they were on in the cold war, step back and sit down and shut up. Anything else was regarded as dangerous neutralism. But these new countries do not believe that they have attained independence to be told that they have only one decision to make, and that a decision on a matter which is not primarily their concern. They are determined to make up their own minds and state their own beliefs. That is another good thing.

The third quality which is common to all the new nations is that they are passionate believers in national independence. It may be difficult for us to understand how strongly they feel. But when I am speaking to people in the United States I remind them that at any rate in that country they should be able to understand, even if they cannot agree. Such views about national independence were fashionable in the United States round about the year 1775. The only difference, of course, was that in America they became emotional and reckless and utterly lacking in responsibility. To use the modern jargon, they even went so far as to resort to violence. Whether we can understand it or not it is a fact that these, the peoples of Asia and Africa, who have been colonial peoples, peoples under the domination of an outside power, are not going to rest content until all colonialism is finished; until the domination of one race by another is brought to an end forever.

The fourth quality which is common to all the new nations is that they are convinced believers in the necessity for an international organization in the form of the United Nations. The big nations will support the United Nations when it suits them; and when it doesn't suit them, as we have ample evidence, they will seek to hamper, hinder and hamstring it. But these, the smaller nations, the poorer nations, the despised nations, have stood by the United Nations. If it were not for them we would not have a United Nations today which was more than an international debating society. When the Russians sought to destroy the initiative of the United Nations by introducing the veto, the troika, into the Secretariat of the United Nations the Americans and the English stood against them and had that been all there would have been just one more disastrous deadlock. But every one of the new nations—not only in one year but for two years running—stood together and made their determined opposition perfectly clear to the Russians. They simply would not have it. And twice the Russians had to withdraw the whole proposal. The new nations are the constant supporters of the United Nations. These are the supporters of the independent initiative of the United Nations.

We are told that if anything disturbs the balance then we're all lost: that at all costs the balance of the bomb must be maintained. It may be so, but it is a miserable prospect for ourselves and for our children and our children's children that we should look to the balance and the bomb as our source of salvation—a sort of deification of defeatism.

Fortunately there is in the world today a new thing—a new idea, a new ideal. In any dispute you still have the two antagonists of two blocks of countries opposing each other, snarling at each other, seeking to weaken, to defeat, to destroy each other. It has happened since the beginning of the world, and it is likely to continue. But now in every dispute there is also a small band of men led by the Secretary-General of the United Nations who bring to each dispute not the tests of national greed or national advantage or national pride, but the tests of international advantage and the benefit of the ordinary people concerned. That is the new thing in the world.

It is exciting to work for the United Nations itself. I spoke to General Rikhye the other day, the Indian Military Adviser to the Secretary-General, who had just come back from New Guinea. In New Guinea the troops during the transitional period there were Pakistanis, and I thought that it might not have been easy for an Indian General in present circumstances to give orders to a Pakistani Brigade. 'There was no difficulty,' General Rikhye replied, 'it was an awkward job we had to do but we are soldiers and we are working for the United Nations—we had not the slightest difference or disagreement.' I myself work for the Special Fund of the United Nations and when I want to report to the Special Fund headquarters I go to see a Frenchman called Paul Marc Henry, one of the leading executive officials of the Fund. He a Frenchman and I an Englishman—after our hour's talk about my expedition to East Africa I walked down the corridor and I reflected that it was unthinkable that either of us should have introduced a British or French interest or motive to our discussion. We would have been ashamed if it had even been suggested. We, a Frenchman and an Englishman, were bringing only the tests for what we could do to help the East African Governments and the peoples of East Africa. I hear talk sometimes of world government. Maybe I do not understand fully what is intended, but I must admit that I am not yet greatly attracted by the thought. Somehow world government suggests to me too many civil servants. But if when we speak of world government we mean the independent and impartial initiative of the Secretary-General, backed by overwhelming international opinion expressed in the parliament of the world—in the General Assembly of the United Nations—we have it—we have it now. It is weak and young and we must not expect too much of it too soon, but if this child is not starved or smothered or strangled by the great powers it will soon grow strong.

In these questions of relations with the nations of Asia and Africa—two-thirds of the population of the world—we can do a certain amount individually; we can do far more by giving our support to the United Nations, the permanent organization devoted to international conciliation and co-operation. The charge I would make against our own leaders is not only that they have by jibe and sneer sought to denigrate the United Nations—the main charge I would make is that they have not sought by every means and at every opportunity to strengthen the United Nations. The United Nations is weak—the organization has weaknesses which would readily be admitted by everyone who serves it. There is a very small band of men on the thirty-eighth floor of the United Nations building coping with many of the main problems of the world. They have no military organization; no intelligence service; practically no money. And yet in each crisis they are expected, usually when everyone else has failed, to find a solution. The danger is that when the time comes to face far greater dangers the United Nations will be too weak and too poor to prevent the division and destruction of the world.

Now let me finish by telling you one of my favourite stories about the United Nations. This concerned Cyprus in 1958. I was at that time in Cyprus, and we were on the brink of civil war throughout the summer months of that year. We then declared our policy and, having done so, it was necessary to show that we would not be deflected from it by violence from either side—and there was violence from both sides at that time. And having declared our policy and shown our initiative and shown our determination to carry it through, then both sides started to shift. First of all the Turks accepted the plan which we put forward and then the Greeks a month or two later declared for independence rather than union with Greece. The Greek government decided, however, to take the matter once more to the United Nations. It had been discussed there in previous years and a favourable vote had been obtained by the Greeks. This time they said they would make their maximum effort; they would seek, by lobbying in all the capitals of the world, to get a two-thirds majority in their favour and thus force Great Britain away from the policy which had been declared. I myself at that time was very unfamiliar with the procedures and manœuvres of the United Nations. We in Cyprus read the long telegrams from New York every night but we did not follow very closely what was going on. The distant debate didn't seem to us to offer any solution of our immediate difficulties. If the Greeks won the vote then it seemed to us we would be further away from a solution and if they lost it there would be no doubt a new outbreak of greater violence. But week by week as the discussion went on in New York we realized that our own delegation was making some progress. This time they had a policy to speak to at least, and in the lobbies and in the capitals of the world we were able to convince one government after another that while our policy might not be perfect at any rate it was an honest attempt, no one could dispute, to find a way out of the miserable situation. The final day came when the vote was to be taken in the General Assembly. The result was now a foregone conclusion. The promises had been given in nearly all the capitals of the world; practically every vote was pledged and it was clear that this time—far from getting their two-thirds majority—the Greeks would not get a majority at all. The resolution which we supported would be passed.

Our Permanent Representative at the United Nations at

that time was Sir Pierson Dixon. He went down on the day of the vote to the United Nations building to what was, of course, a personal triumph. He went down to a great victory in the vote. But he told me later that as he went down that morning he couldn't be content. He thought of us in Cyprus, he knew we were awaiting a new outburst of violence when the vote was taken, that then we would be further away from any solution and any settlement. He told me that a phrase stuck in his mind. He said to himself that what we really needed that day was not a victory but a success.

When he arrived at the United Nations he sent for the Foreign Minister of Turkey and the Foreign Minister of Greece. The Foreign Minister of Turkey came first, Mr. Zorlu. Wasn't it possible even at this last moment to make some new move, not merely to score a victory in the vote but to find some step at least in the direction of a settlement? Mr. Zorlu was not optimistic: he said it would be no use talking to the Greeks—they were in an atmosphere of Greek tragedy. Where was Mr. Averoff, the Foreign Minister of Greece? They discovered that he had gone across New York to meet the Queen of Greece who had arrived on that day. Quickly they got hold of him on the telephone. Would he come down? With the impatient General Assembly awaiting below, the three men—the Foreign Minister of Turkey, the Foreign Minister of Greece and the Ambassador of the United Kingdom met together in the upper room of the United Nations. At the end of half an hour Mr. Averoff and Mr. Zorlu shook hands and pledged each his personal honour to work as rapidly as possible for a final settlement of the Cyprus problem. What to do? They scribbled out a new resolution which meant very little except that neither side had won. Who could propose it? (In the United Nations a sponsor of an existing resolution cannot sponsor another.) They looked anxiously through to find someone who was not in the list of the sponsors of the existing resolutions. Mexico didn't seem to be there. Could they get hold of the Ambassador of Mexico? They put it out on the loudspeakers. The Ambassador of

Mexico hurried in. They asked him if he would move a resolution on Cyprus. Well, he said, he would like to see what it was. They showed him the resolution, they explained the circumstances—quickly he understood, quickly agreed, and without time even to type the resolution they had prepared they went down to the restlessly impatient Assembly. To their astonishment the Assembly saw the Foreign Ministers of Greece and Turkey and the Ambassadors of Mexico and the United Kingdom come together. And then, again to their astonishment, the Ambassador of Mexico, who was not on the list of speakers, had apparently obtained special permission immediately to move a new resolution. They listened to the resolution. They had never heard of it. Each delegate had promised his own country faithfully that he would support one of the resolutions that had previously been put forward. Immediately, to further astonishment, the resolution was supported by the representatives of Great Britain, Greece and Turkey. And that day the resolution passed in the General Assembly unanimously without debate: a very rare occurrence. Within three months we had a settlement.

In these questions of race relations in the modern world and in dealings between the nations we need not think in terms of victories any more. But we badly need some successes.

A Note on the Contributors

STEPHEN WISEMAN, B.Sc., M.Ed., Ph.D., Director and Professor of Education, University of Manchester School of Education.

MISS D. M. LEE, M.A., Ph.D., Reader in Educational Psychology, University of London Institute of Education.

W. D. WALL, B.A., Ph. D., Director of the National Foundation for Educational Research.

HARRY KAY, M.A., Ph.D., Professor of Psychology, University of Sheffield.

BEN MORRIS, B.Sc., Ed.B., Director of the University of Bristol Institute of Education and Professor of Education in the University of Bristol.

W. TAYLOR, B.Sc.(Econ.), Ph.D., Lecturer in Education, University of Oxford Department of Education.

RICHARD HOGGART, M.A., Professor of English and Director of the Centre for Contemporary Cultural Studies, University of Birmingham.

STEPHEN POTTER, Esq., author of *Coleridge and S.T.C.*; *The Muse in Chains*; *Lifemanship*, etc.

SIR HUGH FOOT, G.C.M.G., K.C.V.O., O.B.E., formerly Governor of Jamaica and of Cyprus and U.K. Representative on the Trusteeship Council of the United Nations.

W. R. NIBLETT, B.A., B.Litt., Dean of the University of London Institute of Education and Professor of Education in the University of London.